KING ARTHUR'S

PLACE IN PREHISTORY

KING ARTHUR'S
PLACE IN PREHISTORY
THE GREAT AGE OF
STONEHENGE

W. A. CUMMINS

Bramley Books

A Sutton Publishing Book

Published by Bramley Books
An imprint of Quadrillion Publishing Limited
Godalming Business Centre, Woolsack Way,
Godalming, Surrey GU7 1XW

ISBN 1-85833-769-0

This book was designed and produced by
Alan Sutton Publishing Limited, an imprint of Sutton Publishing Limited,
Phoenix Mill, Thrupp, Stroud, Gloucestershire GL5 2BU

Typeset in 11/14 Bembo.
Typesetting and origination by
Sutton Publishing Limited.
Printed in Great Britain by
WBC Limited, Bridgend.

CONTENTS

List of Illustrations — vii

Acknowledgements — ix

Part I: The Historical Sources

Chapter 1   **The Quest for Arthur** — 3

Chapter 2   **The Dark Ages:** *Arthur Disappears* — 9

Chapter 3   **Stonehenge Connection:** *The Temple of Ambrius* — 24

Chapter 4   **Greek Connection:** *The Hyperboreans* — 34

Part II: Testing the Historical Sources

Chapter 5   **Stonehenge:** *Some Legends Tested* — 45

Chapter 6   **Stones from Ireland:** *Merlin Tested* — 58

Chapter 7   **Greek Contacts:** *The Hyperboreans Tested* — 69

Chapter 8   **Prehistoric Climate:**
                     Diodorus Tested   82

Part III: The Great Age of Stonehenge

Chapter 9   **Merlin:**
                     Architect of Stonehenge   89

Chapter 10   **Stonehenge:**
                     Building Costs   100

Chapter 11   **The Temple of Ambrius:**
                     Religion of the Hyperboreans   117

Chapter 12   **Egyptian Analogy:**
                     Prehistoric Civilization in Britain?   130

Chapter 13   **Prehistoric Pilgrims and the
                     Tourist Trade**   139

Chapter 14   **Who was King Arthur?**   149

Chapter 15   **Vortigern:**
                     Tyrant King and the End of Stonehenge   163

Notes   173

Bibliography   184

Index   189

LIST OF ILLUSTRATIONS

1 *Annales Cambriae*, showing entries for the battles of Badon and Camlann   19

2 Merlin setting a lintel stone in place at Stonehenge   25

3 One of the earliest representations of Stonehenge   28

4 Map of the Aegean   37

5 Stonehenge I, showing excavated portions of the bank, ditch and Aubrey Holes   46

6 Oblique aerial view of Stonehenge from the south-east   47

7 Part of the sarsen circle at Stonehenge, showing the curvature of the lintels   50

8 Grooved bluestone at Stonehenge   52

9 Concentration of Bronze Age round barrows near Stonehenge   54

10 Stonehenge III, showing the surviving standing stones and a few fallen ones   56

11 Map of Pembrokeshire, showing the location of intrusive igneous and volcanic rocks   63

12 Gold ornaments from Wessex Culture burials   70

13 Stone mace and bronze dagger from Bush Barrow   71

14 Gold objects from Wiltshire and Dorset   75

15 Decorative designs from Mycenaean swords   76

16 Map to illustrate the route taken by the prehistoric postal service between the Hyperboreans and the Delians   80

17 A newly excavated Easter Island statue being hauled across country   103

18 Salisbury Plain, showing the principal sites mentioned in the text   106

19 Easter Island statue being raised from the beach   113

20 Bluestone lintel, Stonehenge   114

21 Dolerite axe hammer from Lincolnshire   115

22   The principal stars in the constellation of Cygnus   128
23   Maps of Egypt and Britain   136
24   Oblique aerial view of Avebury from the north   142
25   Stonehenge III from the south-east, as it would have appeared
     to a contemporary observer   146

ACKNOWLEDGEMENTS

In one sense, this book is very much an individual work. I am not a member of a research team, nor do I have much contact with other scholars. In another sense, however, my debt to others is quite beyond measure. Without those great early writers – Diodorus, Herodotus and Homer, in Greece; Manetho, in Egypt; and Nennius, Gildas and Geoffrey of Monmouth, in Britain – this book could never have been conceived. They undertook the immense task of committing the traditions of their people to writing at a time when others were content to pass them on by word of mouth. Then there are the modern scholars who have laboriously translated these early books into modern English, the only language I am able to read. On the two main topics of this book, King Arthur and Stonehenge, my greatest debts are to Professor Leslie Alcock, whose book *Arthur's Britain* has been a source of inspiration, and to Professor R.J.C. Atkinson, whose book on Stonehenge has been an indispensable source ever since it was first published in 1956.

On a more personal note, my family have provided invaluable help and encouragement during the preparation of this book. Judy, Tig, Andrew and Sheila (on a visit from Canada) have all read the book at various stages and made suggestions which resulted in considerable improvements.

Passages quoted from translations of classical and medieval sources are acknowledged as follows: Geoffrey of Monmouth: reprinted by permission of the publishers from *The History of the Kings of Britain* by Geoffrey of Monmouth, translated by Lewis Thorpe (Penguin Classics, 1966) © Lewis Thorpe 1966; Herodotus: reprinted by permission of the publishers from *The Histories* by Herodotus, translated by A. de Selincourt (Penguin Classics, 1954) © The estate of A. de Selincourt; Homer: reprinted by permission of the publishers from *The Iliad* by Homer, translated by E.V. Rieu (Penguin Classics, 1950)

© E.V. Rieu 1950; Gildas: reproduced by kind permission from *Arthurian Period Sources Volume 7, Gildas,* edited by Michael Winterbottom (Phillimore, Chichester, 1978); Nennius: reproduced by kind permission from *Arthurian Period Sources Volume 8, Nennius,* edited by John Morris (Phillimore, Chichester, 1980); Diodorus: reprinted by permission of the publishers and The Loeb Classical Library from *Diodorus of Sicily,* Volumes II and III, translated by C. H. Oldfather (Cambridge, Mass., Harvard University Press, 1935, 1939); the Homeric Hymns: reprinted by permission of the publishers and The Loeb Classical Library from *Hesiod, the Homeric Hymns and Homerica*, translated by H. G. Evelyn White (Cambridge, Mass., Harvard University Press, 1935).

Acknowledgements for the reproduction of photographs are due to the following: illustration 1: BL Harley MS 3859 folio 100a, reproduced by permission of the British Library; 2: BL Egerton MS 3028 folio 30, reproduced by permission of the British Library; 3: Corpus Christi MS 194 folio 57r, reproduced by permission of the Master and Fellows of Corpus Christi College, Cambridge; 6 and 24: reproduced by permission of the Alexander Keiller Museum, R.J.C. Atkinson (Hamish Hamilton, 1956), reprinted by permission of Hamish Hamilton Ltd; 17 and 19: illustrations from *Aku Aku* by Thor Heyerdahl, George Allen & Unwin, now Unwin Hyman of Harper Collins Publishers Ltd, 1958; 21: photograph by John Travis. All line drawings are by the author.

PART I
THE HISTORICAL SOURCES

CHAPTER 1

THE QUEST FOR ARTHUR

The search for King Arthur, the real Arthur, the ultimate inspiration behind the legends, is a bit like looking for the pot of gold at the end of a rainbow. The further back you go, the nearer you approach the object of your enquiry, the less substantial does he seem. Indeed, so shadowy does he become that serious historians have felt obliged to question his very existence. But such is his popular appeal that he has become, for many, the symbol of British survival in the post-Roman period, and books have been written on Arthur's Britain and the Age of Arthur.[1]

In the earliest records, dating originally from the eighth and ninth centuries, Arthur is not a king at all, but a highly successful military leader. He first appears as a king in the early twelfth century, surrounded by a glittering court of dukes, earls and knights, as well as archbishops and bishops. Geoffrey of Monmouth, in his *Historia Regum Britanniae*,[2] written about 1136, tells us that:

> He developed such a code of courtliness in his household that he inspired people living far away to imitate him. The result was that even the man of noblest birth, once he was roused to rivalry, thought nothing of himself unless he wore his arms and dressed like Arthur's knights.

Representing him as a king and supplying him with such a splendid court made Arthur entirely credible to Geoffrey's predominantly aristocratic and military twelfth-century readers. But, for Geoffrey's King Arthur, war and the preparations for war remained the dominant concern and the years of peace are noted in single brief sentences. He is at his magnificent best on the field of battle, when the odds are stacked against him. On the second day of his decisive battle against the Saxons near Bath:

He realized that things were still going well for the enemy and that victory for his own side was not yet in sight. He drew his sword Caliburn, called upon the name of the Blessed Virgin, and rushed forward at full speed into the thickest ranks of the enemy. Every man whom he struck, calling upon God as he did so, he killed at a single blow. He did not slacken his onslaught until he had dispatched four hundred and seventy men with his sword Caliburn. When the Britons saw this, they poured after him in close formation, dealing death on every side.

Some thirteen years later, Arthur decided to invade Gaul, which was at that time under the governorship of a tribune called Frollo. When Arthur had laid siege to Frollo and his army in Paris for a whole month and the Gauls were beginning to suffer from starvation, Frollo, who was a great giant of a man, challenged Arthur to meet him in single combat, so that they could settle their dispute without any further suffering to his people. Both contestants were unhorsed early in the fight and were soon cutting away at each other with their swords. Frollo was the first to find an opening and he struck Arthur on the forehead:

When Arthur saw his leather cuirass and his round shield grow red, he was roused to even fiercer anger. He raised Caliburn in the air with all his strength and brought it down through Frollo's helmet and so on to his head, which he cut into two halves. At this blow Frollo fell to the ground, drummed the earth with his heels and breathed his soul into the winds.

After another nine years of peace, Arthur received a letter from Rome complaining about his tyrannical and criminal behaviour and demanding payment of tribute and submission to Roman overlordship. This was the signal for Arthur's greatest venture of all: an attack on Rome itself. He met a vast Roman army near Autun and engaged it in battle. Once again, at a crucial moment in the battle:

Arthur dashed straight at the enemy. He flung them to the ground and cut them to pieces. Whoever came his way was either killed him-self or had his horse killed under him at a single blow. They ran away from him as sheep run from a fierce lion whom raging hunger compels to devour all that chance throws in his way. Their armour offered them no protection capable of preventing Caliburn, when wielded in the right hand of this mighty King, from forcing them to vomit forth their souls with their life-blood. Ill luck brought two Kings, Sertorius of Libya and Politetes of Bithynia, in Arthur's way. He hacked off their heads and bundled them off to hell. When the Britons saw their King fighting in this way, they became more bold. They charged as one man at the Romans, attacking them in close formation.

After all Arthur's victorious campaigns, the end comes as a terrible anticlimax. But Geoffrey was trying to write history and it was perfectly obvious to him that, far from controlling an empire stretching halfway across Europe, the Britons had long been confined to Wales and other western highland areas. Furthermore his sources made it plain that Arthur himself had fallen at the battle of Camlann. So, in Geoffrey's history, Arthur was busy with the final preparations for the march on Rome, when he heard news of treachery at home. His nephew Mordred had seized the kingdom in his absence and, not only that, but had taken his Queen, Guinevere, as well. Arthur immediately abandoned his expedition and set off for home. In the fateful battle of Camlann, he fought valiantly, but seemingly without the help of his magical sword Caliburn, and in the end was mortally wounded and carried off to the Isle of Avalon, where his wounds could be attended to.

Geoffrey's history contains within it the complete historical framework for all the subsequent legends that grew around the court of King Arthur.[3] A chronological summary of the chief events in the reign of King Arthur, as told by Geoffrey, is given below. The dating of the sequence is taken from Geoffrey's date for the battle of Camlann, one of only three dates given in the whole history.

518 Arthur came to the throne at the age of fifteen and immediately began a campaign against the Saxons, culminating in a decisive battle near Bath. After defeating the Saxons, he reduced the Picts and Scots to submission before the end of the year.

519 Arthur led successful invasions of Ireland and Iceland, and also received the voluntary submission of Gotland and Orkney.

532   Arthur conquered Norway, Denmark and Gaul.

541   Arthur drove an invading Roman army out of Gaul after a great battle near Autun.

542   Arthur returned to fight a civil war in Britain and was mortally wounded at the battle of Camlann.

Geoffrey's history, written in Latin, was immensely successful and over two hundred medieval manuscripts have survived. Within twenty years of its first appearance, it had been translated into French by Wace and, before the end of the century, Layamon had translated the French edition into English. Each translation was accompanied by alterations, additions and omissions, to make it more suitable for the new readers. Finally, before the end of the twelfth century, the great French writer Chretien de Troyes produced a series of romances set in and around Arthur's court. These were not intended as history like Geoffrey's work, but seem to have been the twelfth-century equivalent of historical novels: stories rich in love, adventure and tension, in a historical setting which was sufficiently remote to be idealized as a golden age.

Many of the familiar elements of Arthurian literature were first introduced by the French writers of the twelfth century. The round table was the creation of Wace, in his French translation of Geoffrey's history. The location of Arthur's court at Camelot and the quest for the Holy Grail were both introduced by Chretien de Troyes, together with such important characters as Sir Lancelot, Sir Galahad and Sir Percival. The stories spread right across Europe during the ensuing thirteenth century and continued to develop in England through the fourteenth and fifteenth centuries. A full and beautifully illustrated discussion of the development of Arthurian literature, right up to the present time, is given by Richard Barber in his book, *King Arthur, Hero and Legend*.

To return from literature and the quest for the Holy Grail to history and the quest for King Arthur, an unknown contributor to *The Great Historical, Geographical and Poetical Dictionary*,[4] the first English edition of which was published in 1694, brings us firmly back to earth:

Arthur, a British King, one of the World's nine Worthies, Reign'd as his History tells us, in the beginning of the 6th Age; first he was says Nennius, chief General for the British Kings, in their Wars against the Saxons, but 'tis certain he was more magnified in Songs and Romances, than in true Stories: Besides the 12 great and successful Battels he is said to have fought against the Saxons (the last of which was at Badon-hills) some Historians will have him to have expell'd hence the Saracens, then unknown to Europe; to have Conquer'd Freezland, and all the North-East Isles as far as Russia; and to have made Lapland the Eastern bound of his Empire; but when all these exploits should be done, it does not appear: Certain it is, That he had no rest from the Saxons till after the 12 Battels, and then the Britains, far from seeking Conquests abroad, fell to Civil Wars at home, for which we have Gildas his Testimonies. One would think Policy requir'd of K Arthur, rather to have carried the War into Saxony, to keep the Saxons from coming hither, than to have gone about to Conquer Kingdoms as far as Russia, being scarce able here to defend his own. In short, who this Arthur was, and whether any such ever Reign'd in Britain, has been doubted heretofore, and is by some to this very day.

The situation has changed very little in the last three hundred years! In the present century, Arthur acquired historical respectability in *Roman Britain and the English Settlements*, Volume I of the new *Oxford History of England*, first published in 1936. Professor R.G. Collingwood closed his (Roman Britain) section of the book with a discussion of Arthur's place in history, and reached the conclusion that he was the commander of a mobile cavalry force, which was placed at the disposal of different British Kings as need arose in different parts of the country. His military tactics were modelled either on contemporary Roman practice or on the duties of the former *comes Britanniarum*. In either case, Collingwood concluded that he was 'the last to understand Roman ideas and use them for the good of the British people . . . and the story of Roman Britain ends with him'.[5]

More recently, there has been a great deal of archaeological activity at various sites more or less connected with King Arthur: at Tintagel, on the north Cornish cliffs, Arthur's birthplace in Geoffrey's history; at South Cadbury Castle, a hill-fort near the Dorset–Somerset border, which has been identified as the site of Arthur's court at Camelot; at

Glastonbury, where Arthur's tomb was supposed to have been discovered in 1190, and which has since then been identified with Avalon; and at many other sites. In *The Quest for Arthur's Britain*, published in 1968,[6] Geoffrey Ashe shows that all these sites have yielded artefacts dating from the sub-Roman or dark-age period, roughly between AD 400 and 650. This archaeological work has told us a great deal about the period but, almost inevitably, absolutely nothing about Arthur himself. This was followed, in 1971, by Leslie Alcock's *Arthur's Britain*, the title of which would seem to imply that the quest had been successful. Alcock begins his book with a critical discussion of the documentary evidence, from which he concludes that 'Arthur was an authentic person . . . most probably a king or prince, but if not that, then emphatically a great warrior.'[7] The rest of the book is concerned with the history and archaeology of the period from AD 367 to 634. Finally, John Morris, in *The Age of Arthur*, published in 1973, had no doubts about Arthur. For him, Arthur 'was as real as Alfred the Great or William the Conqueror; and his impact upon future ages mattered as much or more so', and he reigned for some twenty years over a Roman-style empire in Britain.[8] The book covers the period from AD 350 to 650.

The pendulum has now started to swing back in the other direction. D.N. Dumville, in an article published in 1977, strongly criticized what he called the 'Arthurian' approach to the problems of fifth- and sixth-century British history, which he attributed to a 'no smoke without fire' school of thought. His view is that the written evidence, which 'is remarkably slight until a very late date, shows Arthur as a figure of legend'.[9] As a direct result of this article, Peter Salway, in *Roman Britain*, Volume IA in the latest series of *The Oxford History of Britain*, now says 'I personally am not prepared to say whether Arthur was a real person or not – least of all whether he was a national British leader who fought battles at identifiable places and had a capital that can be placed on a map.'[10]

How right was that unknown contributor to *The Great Geographical, Historical and Poetical Dictionary* three hundred years ago. Arthur flits like a ghost across the pages of history, with some people believing in him and others not, and no one absolutely certain either way. This is dangerous ground, and a new interpretation is attempted in the pages which follow, not because any new evidence has come to light, but simply because we may not have been asking the right questions.

CHAPTER 2

THE DARK AGES: ARTHUR DISAPPEARS

There is one British writer who, above all others, ought to be considered an authority on the 'Arthurian period' of British history. Gildas, the author of *De Excidio Britonum*,[1] was born, as he himself tells us, in the same year as the siege of Badon Hill, and he died about the year 570. He was probably writing within a few years of the battle of Camlann. For the first half of the sixth century, his evidence ought to stand supreme. He was there. That he is not the most popular authority for the period may be attributed, at least in part, to the fact that he totally fails to mention Arthur! What he does have to say, however, is of the greatest interest. After describing the ravages of the Saxon invaders and how the native British were holding out in the hills and forests and on the sea cliffs, he comes to the rallying of the British resistance:

> Their leader was Ambrosius Aurelianus, a gentleman who, perhaps alone of the Romans, had survived the shock of this notable storm: certainly his parents, who had worn the purple, were slain in it. His descendants in our day have become greatly inferior to their grandfather's excellence. Under him our people regained their strength, and challenged the victors to battle. The Lord assented, and the battle went their way. From then on victory went now to our countrymen, now to their enemies . . . This lasted right up to the year of the siege of Badon Hill, pretty well the last defeat of the villains, and certainly not the least. That was the year of my birth: as I know, one month of the forty-fourth year since then has already passed. But the cities of our land are not populated even now as they once were; right to the present they are deserted, in ruins and unkempt. External wars may have stopped, but not civil ones.

Whatever else it was, this period of British history was not a golden age. The desertion and decay of the cities, described by Gildas, is consistent with the archaeological evidence.[2] This is not the setting for King Arthur's conquest of Gaul, even less for his attempt on Rome. In so far as it is possible to read this passage without any preconceived ideas, Ambrosius Aurelianus appears as a man who exactly fits Collingwood's description of Arthur as the last of the Romans. He came from an aristocratic Roman (Romano-British) family and, when the need arose, established himself as the natural leader and united the British against their common enemy. Gildas seems to imply, though he certainly does not explicitly state it, that Ambrosius was in command throughout the campaign, right up to the decisive siege of Badon Hill, and that when he died, there was no one of sufficient stature to maintain the unity that he had been able to establish. There hardly seems room for Arthur's career in Britain here, let alone his overseas campaigns.

The earliest authority for Arthur's military reputation is the *Historia Brittonum*,[3] originally compiled early in the ninth century probably by Nennius, whose preface, preserved in some manuscripts, contains the statement that he was a pupil of the holy Elvodug (Elfoddw, Bishop of Bangor, died 809). He describes his book as 'a heap of all that I have found, both from the Annals of the Romans and from the Chronicles of the Holy Fathers, and from the writings of the Irish and the English, and out of the traditions of our elders'. Nennius mentions Ambrosius once or twice and calls him 'the great king among all the kings of the British nation', a description which tallies with what Gildas tells us about him. Of Arthur, he has more to say:

Then Arthur fought against them in those days, together with the kings of the British; but he was their leader in battle. The first battle was at the mouth of the river called Glein. The second, the third, the fourth and the fifth were on another river, called the Douglas, which is in the country of Lindsey.[4] The sixth battle was on the river called Bassas. The seventh battle was in the Caledonian Forest, that is, Cat Coit Celidon. The eighth battle was in Guinnion fort, and in it Arthur carried the image of the holy Mary, the everlasting Virgin, on his shield,[5] and the heathen were put to flight on that day, and there was a great slaughter upon them, through the power of Our Lord

Jesus Christ and the power of the holy Virgin Mary, his mother. The ninth battle was fought in the city of the Legion. The tenth battle was on the river called Tribruit. The eleventh battle was on the hill called Agned. The twelfth battle was on Badon Hill and in it nine hundred and sixty men fell in one day, from a single charge of Arthur's, and no one laid them low save he alone; and he was victorious in all his campaigns.

It is generally agreed that the Arthurian passage in the *Historia Brittonum* 'is a Latin prose rendering of an Old Welsh battle-catalogue-poem',[6] a poem which had been transmitted orally for over 250 years before being committed to writing. None of the battles listed can be located with absolute certainty,[7] though the battle of Badon Hill is of particular interest in view of its historical importance, vouched for by Gildas. But here lies the problem. In the battle poem preserved by Nennius, Arthur's career stretches backwards from Badon, through a long series of battles; whereas in Gildas' account, the career of Ambrosius reaches forward, through a long series of battles, towards Badon. It is as if they were one and the same person. There can be little reasonable doubt which of these two, the priest (Gildas) or the poet, is the more reliable source for the period.

Gildas was *writing* for the kings and princes of his own time and telling them, in no uncertain terms, exactly what he thought of them. Ambrosius Aurelianus is held up to them as an example of old fashioned Roman virtues, much as in our own time we are not infrequently lectured on Victorian values or Victorian morality. Gildas could not afford to make mistakes. His readers would have known all about Ambrosius. Their fathers and grandfathers would have fought alongside him against the Saxons. Furthermore, his account has the ring of truth about it: 'from then on victory went now to our countrymen, now to the enemy'.

The poet, on the other hand, was *reciting* (as opposed to writing) for the entertainment of his audience, telling and retelling the tales of old, when Britain was great and her leaders, cast in a heroic mould, were as ready to slay a dragon as to slaughter the enemy in their hundreds on the field of battle. At Badon Hill, 'nine hundred and sixty men fell in one day, from a single charge of Arthur's, and no one laid them low save he alone; and he was victorious in all his campaigns.' There is poetic licence, whatever prosaic interpretation we may be persuaded to put on this passage. After 250 years, it is perhaps a wonder that there is any vestige of historical fact left in the poem, but Badon Hill is not only there but presented correctly as the culmination of a long series of battles.

Why is the poem about Arthur and not about Ambrosius Aurelianus? Was Ambrosius too Roman to be a real British hero? Were the leaders who followed him jealous of his fame? Did the kings who were at the receiving end of Gildas' invective say in effect to their minstrels, 'Don't you dare sing songs about Ambrosius at my court'? Did his name not fit readily into the verse pattern in use at the time? Did all his achievements simply get absorbed into an already flourishing Arthurian legend? These are some of the possibilities.

The poem begins with the words 'then Arthur fought against them in those days, together with the kings of the Britons'. If Arthur was already a legendary hero, this would be understood to mean 'then Arthur (returned and) fought against them in those days, together with the kings of the Britons'. Everyone would have known that this was simply a poetic way of saying that something almost miraculous had happened: everyone, that is, for the first few generations. After a century or two, no one would have had the slightest idea that the Arthur of the poem was not the real flesh and blood victor of Badon. The miracle, of course, was uniting the kings of the Britons in a common cause. It happened again some seven hundred years later, under the leadership of Llewellyn the Great, and is referred to by the Welsh historian, A.H. Williams,[8] as 'the almost impossible feat of uniting them all in fierce opposition to his (King John's) new policy of wholesale conquest and subjugation'.

The account of King Arthur's early British battles given by Geoffrey of Monmouth bears some interesting resemblances to the battle poem in the *Historia Brittonum*. Unlike Nennius, Geoffrey did not make a heap of all that he collected, but attempted to blend his material into a narrative history. Summarizing King Arthur's battles from Geoffrey's history, we obtain the following sequence: (i) river Douglas; (ii) siege of York; (iii) Kaerliudcoit, on a hill between two rivers in the district of Lindsey (and identified by Geoffrey as Lincoln); (iv) Caledonian wood; (v) Bath (clearly Geoffrey's interpretation of Badon), involving the storming of a hilltop held by the Saxons. This last battle lasted two days and King

Arthur, carrying a shield bearing the image of the Virgin Mary, killed 470 men in a single charge.

Clearly these battles were not derived from Nennius. The first battle, at the mouth of the river Glein, is missing; there is only one battle on the river Douglas, and none on the river Bassas; and the four battles between the Caledonian wood and Badon Hill are all missing. Similarly, Geoffrey records two battles not listed by Nennius: the siege of York and the battle of Kaerliudcoit. Furthermore, Nennius had Arthur kill 960 men in a single charge at Badon, whereas in Geoffrey's account, this number is reduced to 470. Finally, the shield bearing the image of the Virgin Mary is carried at different battles in the two accounts.

It is equally certain that Geoffrey did not invent his story. The clearest indication that he was using an earlier source is given by his attempt to interpret the name Kaerliudcoit. While the differences make it clear that his source was not Nennius, the similarities are none the less striking: the river Douglas, the district of Lindsey, the Caledonian wood, Badon, the shield with the image of the Virgin Mary on it, the hundreds of men killed in a single charge by Arthur alone. Geoffrey and Nennius were independently using different versions of the same poem listing Arthur's battles. As a historical document in the strict sense, this poem has very limited value, and its importance has been greatly exaggerated because of the shortage of other early sources. A well known modern example will serve to illustrate the point.

> The Grand old Duke of York,
> He had ten thousand men.
> He marched them up to the top of the hill
> And he marched them down again.

We know, from independent historical sources, that the Duke in the song was the second son of George III and was commander-in-chief of the British army in a disastrous winter campaign in the Netherlands in 1794.[9] Before his defeat, he had been sent reinforcements of ten thousand men. But if we try to use the song itself as a historical source, the matter is not so simple. We might for example try to find out which hill the Duke of York had his men march up and down to so little effect. In the course of this enquiry we might note that, during the present century, schoolchildren have been heard singing the same song about Napoleon and a very similar one about the Kaiser.[10] Even more interesting is a variant recorded 150 years before the time of Napoleon and the Grand old Duke of York:

> The King of France went up the hill
> With forty thousand men.
> The King of France came down the hill,
> And ne'er went up again.

As long ago as 1645, it was reported that this song referred to King Henry IV of France, who raised an army of forty thousand men not long before he was assassinated in 1610. The Grand old Duke of York may never have marched his men up a hill at all (he may not even have found a hill in the Netherlands!). He acquired a traditional song and has had the misfortune to be stuck with it ever since. The song has been circulating for over 350 years and the printed version has crystallized just one brief moment in its long history.

To return to Arthur's battles, there are some forty surviving medieval manuscripts of the *Historia Brittonum* and they display no significant variations in the battle poem. This must certainly not be taken to imply that this was the true or indeed the only version of the poem. It simply means that, by incorporating it in his history, Nennius preserved one particular version of the poem for posterity. Geoffrey also, in his own way, preserved another. By the time they were writing, neither Nennius nor Geoffrey had any reason to suppose that their version of the poem was not a valid source for the history they were trying to compile.

Geoffrey of Monmouth, unlike Nennius, takes Arthur's career beyond the battle of Badon Hill and indeed beyond the confines of Britain. We in the twentieth century, with our accumulated knowledge of history, can be fairly sure that there was no British invasion of Gaul in the sixth century, whether by Arthur or anyone else. For Geoffrey too, such an invasion must have posed problems, familiar as he was with the works of Gildas and Bede.[11] Either he was writing a work of fiction and paying scant regard to historical veracity (a fairly common view of Geoffrey's work), or he must have had some compelling reason for introducing this episode, perhaps a source now lost to us. The question at issue here is not whether there was or was not a British invasion of Gaul at this time (we are fairly certain of the answer to that one), but whether or not Geoffrey had good reason to believe that there was such an invasion.

The gratuitous invention of lost historical sources should not be undertaken lightly, but nor should a twelfth-century history be rejected because some of the events it describes are incompatible with the facts as we understand them today. The history of one of the few sources we do have for this period might serve to give us a sense of perspective in the matter. The battle poem discussed above was collected by Nennius, translated into Latin, and incorporated into his history. It was faithfully copied by scribes down the centuries and has been preserved for us in some forty medieval manuscripts. During the present century, it has been reproduced in many printed volumes and is a familiar source to all students of the period. We would know nothing whatever of the former existence of this poem had not one man, Nennius, taken the trouble to translate it and include it in his book. It would never have been recognized from the narrative account given by Geoffrey. How many more such poems were there, of which we have no written record at all?

It has been suggested that Geoffrey's account of King Arthur's overseas campaigns was modelled on a late fourth-century invasion of Gaul under the leadership of the Roman general Magnus Maximus.[12] In 383, Magnus, who came from Spain and had served in Britain for a number of years, led a British army into Gaul against the western Roman emperor, Gratian. The Gaulish army soon deserted to him, thus enabling him to achieve a bloodless conquest. Gratian was killed soon afterwards. For the next four years, Magnus ruled over the north-western part of the Roman empire, comprising the provinces of Britain, Gaul and Spain. Then he decided to invade Italy. He crossed the Alps and took Milan without meeting any opposition, but was finally defeated and killed in 388, in Pannonia, in the vicinity of what is now the border between Italy and Yugoslavia.[13]

Geoffrey was of course fully aware of Magnus Maximus and his invasion of Gaul. His own account of Magnus is strongly influenced by Gildas, one of his acknowledged historical sources. Gildas blamed Magnus for denuding Britain of her legions and the flower of her youth, and thus leaving her wide open to the inroads of the Picts, Scots and

other heathen races. As a result, he did not have a good word to say
about him:

> The throne of his wicked empire he placed at Trier, whence he raged
> so madly against his masters that of the two legitimate emperors he
> drove one from Rome, the other from his life – which was a very
> holy one. Soon, though entrenched in these appalling acts of daring,
> he had his evil head cut off at Aquilea – he who had in a sense, cast
> down the crowned heads that ruled the whole world.[14]

Geoffrey describes Magnus as obsessed with power, greedy, inhuman
and savage. The slaughter he caused in Gaul was so great that large parts
of the country had to be restocked with people from Britain. 'He set up
the capital of his empire at Treves [Trier]. Then he vented his fury upon
the two Emperors Gracianus and Valentinianus, killing the one and dri-
ving the second from Rome.'[15]

It seems unlikely that Geoffrey would knowingly have used any part
of the evil career of Magnus Maximus to add lustre to his great hero,
King Arthur. There are, none the less, striking resemblances between
Geoffrey's account of the Arthurian invasion of Gaul and the actual invasion by Magnus Maximus. The most notable of these is the almost
bloodless conquest. In Geoffrey's account of King Arthur's invasion, 'the
better part of the army of the Gauls was already in Arthur's service, for
he had bought them over by the gifts he had given them.'[16] For
Geoffrey, who revelled in accounts of battle lines and heavy losses inflict-
ed on both sides, such a peaceful achievement of a military objective
must have seemed very uninspiring. He made up for it by having Frollo,
the commander of the Gaulish army, killed by Arthur in a splendid one-
to-one fight, instead of having him assassinated, as was probably the fate
of Gratian.

Gildas, as we have seen, had a very low opinion of Magnus Maximus
and blamed him, probably quite wrongly, for the weakened state of
Britain in the succeeding century. Others remembered the achievements
of Magnus: the fact that he had started from Britain and become Roman
Emperor in the west. His Spanish origin was forgotten and he became
an honorary Briton, a Briton of such famous memory that he was credited with being the ancestor of more than one royal line.[17] If the gen-

uine achievements of Ambrosius Aurelianus could be attached to the hypothetical legendary hero, Arthur, so also could those of Magnus Maximus. If Geoffrey had them in this form, he would not have recognized their origin and would have felt bound to use them, despite their apparent conflict with the evidence of Gildas. In other words, the fiction which Geoffrey created could have been based on what he conceived to be sound historical fact.

Geoffrey's King Arthur does not, like Magnus Maximus, meet his end on foreign soil, but returns home to civil war and the battle of Camlann. For this, his final battle, the historical source is the *Annales Cambriae*:

537   The battle of Camlann, in which Arthur and Medraut perished, and there was plague in Britain and Ireland.[18]

Twenty-one years earlier is an entry for the battle of Badon Hill:

516   The battle of Badon, in which Arthur carried the cross of our Lord Jesus Christ on his shield[19] for three days and three nights and the Britons were the victors.

The Annales Cambriae were first assembled in their present form in the second half of the tenth century, when they were copied from annals, which had been kept at St Davids since the late eighth century. Earlier entries, back to the middle of the fifth century, were entered retrospectively from Irish annals and from North Welsh/North British annals.[20] The annals in the four surviving medieval manuscripts, the originals of which were copied independently and at different dates from the growing series of annals at St Davids, are not provided with dates (AD), and there is no reason to suppose that the lost annals at St Davids had dates.[21] The years are given in three vertical columns, each one being marked as 'an' and the decades counted as 'an x', 'an xx', 'an xxx', etc., from the beginning of the sequence. The dates have been supplied by modern editors, who have calibrated the annals using events which can be dated from independent sources, and these dates are used in the present discussion.

The entry for the battle of Badon Hill is potentially of the greatest importance: giving a date for the siege recorded by Gildas and confirm-

ing the connection of this important battle with Arthur. There is however a serious difficulty. The battle of Badon is dated to the year 516,
thirty-one years before the death of Maelgwn, King of Gwynedd, in the
year 547. But Maelgwn (Maglocunus) was one of the four kings to
whom, in particular, Gildas was addressing his tirade in *De Excidio
Britonum*. It follows that Gildas cannot have been writing after 547 and
that the battle of Badon, which took place in the year of his birth forty-
three years earlier, must have been fought in or before 504. An error of
twelve years, at the very least, is unacceptable if we are to treat these
annals as being derived from sources contemporary with the events they
record, and if we cannot treat them as such they lose much of their value
as historical sources. Either Gildas or the *Annales Cambriae* is providing
us with incorrect information. The problem is to decide which.

The first possibility to be considered is that Gildas may have been mis-
taken when he said that 'the year of the siege of Badon Hill . . . was the
year of my birth; as I know, one month of the forty-fourth year since
then has already passed.' He is, however, hardly likely to have said he
was forty-three years old, when he was in fact no more than thirty-one.
When considering his statement that the siege of Badon Hill took place
in the year of his birth, we have to remember that, at the time Gildas
was writing, no one thought in terms of dates as we know them. A
chronological framework, in so far as it was required at all, was provided
by important events or by the succession in some relatively stable dynasty
or government. This is well illustrated by the chronological calculations
which precede the *Annales Cambriae*:

> . . . And from the [beginning of the] reign of Vortigern to the quar-
> rel between Vitalinus and Ambrosius are 12 years, that is Wallop,
> the battle of Wallop. Vortigern, however held empire in Britain in
> the consulship of Theodosius and Valentinian, and in the fourth
> year of his reign the English came to Britain in the consulship of
> Felix and Taurus, in the 400th year from the Passion[22] of our Lord
> Jesus Christ. From the year when the English came to Britain and
> were welcomed by Vortigern to [the consulship of] Decius and
> Valerian are 69 years.[23]

There is not the slightest reason to doubt Gildas' statements that he

Annales Cambriae showing entries for the battles of Badon (*an lxxii*) and Camlann (*an xciii*) in the right-hand column

was born in the year of the siege of Badon Hill and that he was forty-three years old at the time of writing. This leaves us with the entries in the *Annales Cambriae*.

By far the most abundant events recorded in the annals are deaths (120) and more than a quarter of them give the circumstance of death: killed in a named battle (13), killed, often by some enemy such as the Saxons (12), drowned (2), poisoned (2), died in Rome (2), beheaded (1). The entry for the year 547, 'A great plague in which Maelgwn, king of Gwynedd died', presents no problems. The great plague and the death of a king as important as Maelgwn were both events which one would expect to find in contemporary annals.

Next to deaths, the most frequently recorded events are battles, slaughters, invasions, hammerings and devastations (53). Of the named battles (29), only just over half the entries (15) provide any further information: one or more deaths in the battle (9), names of the leaders or peoples involved (8), names of the victorious leader or people (5). Some entries (7) provide more than one of these details. Some examples are given below:

573 The battle of Arfderydd between the sons of Eliffer and Gwenddolau son of Ceidio; in which battle Gwenddolau fell.

613 The battle of Caer Legion and there fell Selyf son of Cynan.

630 On the Kalends of January the battle of Meigen; and there Edwin was killed with his two sons; but Cadwallon was the victor.

631 The battle of Cantscaul in which Cadwallon fell.

722 The battle of Hehil among the Cornish, the battle of Garth Maelog, the battle of Pencon among the south Britons, and the Britons were the victors in those battles.

728 The battle of Mount Carno.

750 Battle between the Picts and the Britons, that is the battle of Mocetauc. And their king Talorgan is killed by the Britons.[24]

Historical significance is not one of the strong points of these battle entries. The battle of Meigen in 630 is the only one which suggests a British victory over the Saxons. This is also the only battle for which a date is given within the year. The three British victories recorded in 722 seem a little hollow, since no one else seems to have been involved! It seems likely that all these battles and most of the other events in the annals were recorded, in the first instance, as part of the chronological framework: memorable events which would serve as time markers, rather than records which would be of historical interest in an established dating scheme.

The entry for the battle of Badon is completely out of character with these generally terse battle records:'The battle of Badon, in which Arthur carried the Cross of our Lord Jesus Christ for three days and nights on his shield and the Britons were the victors.'

The simplest solution to the dating problem would be that the whole of the Badon entry was added to the annals long after the event and placed (unwittingly) in the wrong year. The character of the entry clearly points to another version of the poem listing Arthur's battles as the source of the information. Instead of the image of the Virgin Mary, we have the Cross of Jesus Christ and, instead of Geoffrey of Monmouth's two-day battle, we have a three-day battle; but these are minor details.

Before this suggestion can be accepted, there are some supplementary questions which must be answered: (i) Why was the battle of Badon not entered at the time? (ii) Why was it added later? (iii) When was it added? (iv) How was its (incorrect) date fixed? Before attempting to answer these questions, it is necessary to consider the battle of Camlann and the death of Arthur.

Unlike Badon, there is nothing unusual about the Camlann entry in the *Annales Cambriae*:

537 The battle of Camlann, in which Arthur and Medraut fell.

There seems to be no good reason why the deaths of Arthur and Medraut in the battle of Camlann should not be accepted as based on contemporary evidence. At the end of three chapters of very full discussion of the evidence, Leslie Alcock concludes that this is 'the irreducible minimum of historical fact', which assures us 'that Arthur was an authentic person'.[25]   This is perfectly true, so long as Arthur means no more than the Arthur who fell in the battle of Camlann.   Anyone who has ever studied genealogy will be well aware of the danger of confusing different individuals who just happen to have the same name.

There were a few other British Arthurs around during this period. There was Arthur map Petr, a member of the royal family of Dyfed, who may have been born towards the end of the sixth century; and Artuir son of Aedan, King of Dalriada, who was killed in the battle of the Miathi, towards the end of the seventh century.[26]   These, and other examples, are usually taken to mean that the fame of Arthur ('the Arthur') was making the name popular.   This is perfectly possible, but how can we know whether the Arthur who was killed at Camlann was 'the Arthur' or one of the other Arthurs named after him?   The answer is that we cannot know for sure.   Bearing this in mind, we can now return to the later insertion of the Badon entry and the questions raised in connection with this.

Possible locations for Badon are all in southern or eastern England,[27] which could explain why the battle went unrecorded by the early North Welsh/North British annalist.   Whoever inserted the Badon entry was aware of the importance of that battle from Gildas and knew of the fame of Arthur from the battle poem.   Finding a record of Arthur's death at Camlann, he assumed that this referred to the Arthur of Badon and accordingly placed his Badon entry in the annals at an appropriate time interval before Camlann. The most likely date for this insertion would be sometime in the late eighth century, when the St Davids annals were being set up, and early material was being culled from such sources as were available.   If this is really what happened, then this unknown St Davids annalist made an important contribution to the Arthurian legend.

The Arthurian legend has grown and developed over the centuries to satisfy the needs of each succeeding age.   Geoffrey of Monmouth's Arthur, who had such tremendous appeal in the twelfth century, was quite different from the Arthur of the sixth century and equally different from the fifteenth-century Arthur of Sir Thomas Malory.   The legend has evolved, is perhaps still evolving, and now, with our insatiable curiosity, we want to know how it all started.   Is there any valid reason why the earliest documentary evidence for Arthur should actually be a record of the ultimate source of the legend? Is it not just as likely that the sixth-century Arthur represents the contemporary stage in the evolution of the legend, rather than its actual origin, like a still from a motion picture of the Arthurian legend through time? It has been shown in this chapter that this is a very real possibility; by no means a certainty, but a possibility which accords well with the available documentary evidence, which avoids any awkward clashes with Gildas, and which allows us to treat Geoffrey of Monmouth with a little more respect than he is usually accorded.

CHAPTER 3

STONEHENGE CONNECTION: THE TEMPLE OF AMBRIUS

King Arthur as a legendary hero in prehistoric Britain would be a bit like Odysseus without Homer: a hero without a biographer. Gildas, writing in the sixth century AD, is the first native British writer whose works have come down to us. How many more heroes might have been known to us, if only some British Homer had been there to record their deeds a thousand years before. The situation looks bleak, but is not quite as bad as it seems.

Nennius, in his preface, refers to 'the traditions of our elders'. Geoffrey of Monmouth, in the first paragraph of his dedication, praises the works of Gildas and Bede and wonders at the lack of other works on the early kings of Britain:

> Yet the deeds of these men were such that they deserve to be praised for all time. What is more, these deeds were handed joyfully down in oral tradition, just as if they had been committed to writing, by many peoples who had only their memory to rely on.[1]

In the absence of any other source of information, we must make do with such snippets of tradition as may have been preserved for us by Nennius and Geoffrey. It is either that or abandon the quest altogether; and abandoning quests is not in the Arthurian tradition.

In the half century or so immediately preceding the reign of King Arthur, Geoffrey of Monmouth gives an account of Vortigern and the arrival of the Saxons, under the leadership of Hengest and Horsa; Aurelius Ambrosius and his resistance to the Saxon advance; and Utherpendragon and his civil war. Spanning the whole of this period is the extraordinary presence of Merlin: prophet, counsellor, magician, healer, engineer and architect. With Merlin we are, in one sense at least, on fairly firm ground. History is silent about him. Even *The Great Historical, Geographical and Poetical Dictionary* of 1694 has nothing to say on the subject.[2] The brief statement in the *Annales Cambriae*, under the year 573, that 'Merlin went mad' has caused hardly a murmur in academic circles. Merlin is a legendary figure and his legend, like that of King Arthur, is still flourishing, as indicated by such recent titles as *The Quest for Merlin* and *The Mystic Life of Merlin*.[3]

From the historical point of view, the great interest of Merlin is that he is credited with the building, or rather the re-erection on its present site, of Stonehenge. He had the stones shipped over from Ireland and set up as a memorial to the victims of a treacherous massacre by Hengest and his Saxons. Thereafter Stonehenge became a burial place for the kings of Britain. Geoffrey records the burial there of Ambrosius Aurelius, Arthur's uncle; Utherpendragon, his father, and Constantine, his cousin and successor.

In Geoffrey's history, then, we have the great legendary figure of

Merlin setting a lintel stone in place at Stonehenge, from a
fourteenth-century French manuscript

Merlin and the unquestionably prehistoric site of Stonehenge linked together across the second half of the fifth century and the first half of the sixth century AD. There can be no doubt that Geoffrey's history is wrong here, but our concern is less with this so-called 'Arthurian period' of British history than with the legends which may have become attached to it from earlier times. The question we need to ask is not whether Geoffrey's history is accurate or not, in the light of modern research, but whether he invented the stories about Merlin and Stonehenge or derived them from sources which he considered reliable (or at least the best available).

The Stonehenge–Merlin story begins with the treacherous massacre of the British leaders by Hengest and his Saxons, an event which was certainly not invented by Geoffrey. An earlier account of this massacre is to be found at the end of the *Kentish Chronicle* in the *Historia Brittonum*.[4] This chronicle is a British account of the middle years of the fifth century, when the Britons lost control of Kent. It begins with the arrival of the brothers, Hengest and Horsa. Vortigern welcomed them and granted them the Isle of Thanet, while they agreed to fight against his enemies, the Picts and the Scots. The Saxons' numbers were soon swelled by further immigration from their homelands and Vortigern became fatally involved with them by marrying the beautiful daughter of Hengest, for whose hand he granted her father the whole of Kent, seemingly oblivious of the fact that this might upset the British King of Kent, Gwyrangon. Vortigern's sons, Vortimer and Cateyrn, who may have disapproved of their new stepmother as much as of their father's high-handed behaviour, led a British army of resistance against the Saxon domination of Kent. For a time they were successful and besieged the Saxons in the Isle of Thanet. Then Horsa and Cateyrn were killed in battle and, not long afterwards, Vortimer died. Hengest asked Vortigern to arrange a peace conference and it was agreed that the two sides should meet, unarmed, to confirm the peace treaty:

But Hengest told his followers to hide their daggers under their feet in their shoes, saying 'When I call out to you and say "English, draw your knives", take your daggers from your shoes and fall upon them, and stand firm against them. But do not kill the king; keep him alive for my daughter's sake, whom I wedded to him, for it is better for us that he be ransomed from us.' So the conference assembled, and the

English, friendly in their words, but wolfish in heart and deed, sat down, like allies, man beside man. Hengest cried out as he had said, and all three hundred Seniors of king Vortigern were murdered, and the king alone was taken and held prisoner. To save his life, he ceded several districts, namely Essex and Sussex, together with Middlesex and other districts that they chose and designated.[5]

Geoffrey's account differs from this in several respects. He records a death toll of about four hundred and sixty counts and earls and then, almost as an afterthought, says that some of the Britons managed to defend themselves with sticks and stones and that Eldol, Count of Gloucester, laid about him with a wooden stake and killed seventy men before he left the scene of the disaster. He does not mention Essex, Sussex or Middlesex, but simply that Vortigern conceded all that they demanded. From our point of view, the most significant difference is that he gives the location of the peace conference as the Cloister of Ambrius, 'not far from Kaercaradduc, which is now called Salisbury', and later described as a monastery of three hundred brethren, founded by Ambrius many years before.[6]

The dispute which preceded the peace conference was confined to Kent. Did the fateful meeting between the British and Saxon leaders really take place at an otherwise unknown monastery on Salisbury Plain? Did Geoffrey simply invent his location for the conference, and if so why? Or did he have good reason for believing that the massacre was indeed perpetrated at his Cloister of Ambrius?

It seems, on the face of it, highly improbable that the conference should have been arranged so far from Kent. Hengest, with his own mind already bent on treachery, would hardly have agreed to a meeting so far inside enemy territory, for fear of being caught in a trap himself.

If Geoffrey invented the Cloister of Ambrius, he presumably derived its name from Amesbury, some two-and-a-half miles east of Stonehenge, which was originally called Ambresbyrig. His reason for bringing it into his history must have been to provide an introduction for the subsequent, and presumably equally fictitious, building of Stonehenge. In Geoffrey's history,[7] the victims of the massacre were buried in the cemetery adjacent to the Cloister of Ambrius and the burial service was conducted by the Bishop of Gloucester. Some years later, when peace had been restored, Aurelius Ambrosius visited the site and resolved to build a

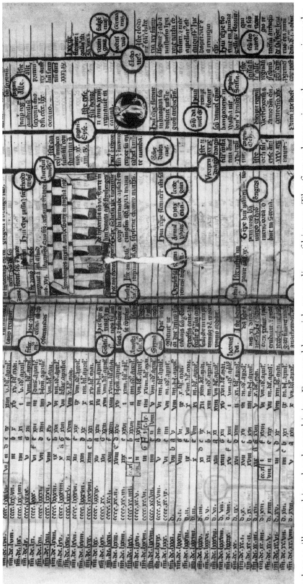

Stonehenge illustrated in a book combining Easter tables with an outline of history. The first column gives the years since the Creation and the second column the years AD. The next few columns are devoted to the calculation of the date of Easter. The circles on the first thick vertical line contain the names of successive popes. The vertical line to the right of Stonehenge has the names of two kings of Britain, Aurelius Ambrosius and Utherpendragon. Beneath Stonehenge, in the year AD 491, is a brief account of the Giant's Ring being brought over from Ireland. The historical details are from Geoffrey of Monmouth. From a fourteenth-century French manuscript.

monument to the memory of those who had fallen. After failing to find a suitable design, he finally called upon Merlin, who recommended fetching the Giant's Ring over from Ireland and setting it up around the graves of the dead.

Utherpendragon was sent off to Ireland, with an army of fifteen thousand men, to collect the stones from the Giant's Ring. The Irish king, Gillomanius, gathered an army to resist him, but was soon defeated and forced to flee, leaving his men 'either mangled or killed outright' on the field of battle. To the twentieth-century reader this seems an outrageous act of robbery with violence, carried out entirely for the purpose of commemorating the victims of a considerably smaller outrage; and the Irish were entirely innocent in the matter. The Britons then proceeded to the Giant's Ring, where Merlin 'placed in position all the gear he considered necessary and dismantled the stones more easily than you could believe'. They were then shipped back to England and re-erected round the burial place. It must have required all Merlin's skill to set up those great stones around the graves of the 460 victims of the massacre: graves which could have been no more than about ten years old.

Of course Stonehenge was not built in the shadow of a monastery. It stands by itself and always has done. It is magnificent in its isolation and the whole effect would have been ruined by setting it up beside a monastery large enough to accommodate 300 monks. So why invent the Cloister of Ambrius? Why not just have the meeting on the open plain, not far from Salisbury, and then have Stonehenge erected on the site of the massacre by itself, as it really is, and as it really was in the twelfth century too? The idea that Geoffrey invented the Cloister of Ambrius as the site for the peace treaty and massacre is seriously flawed. It does nothing to improve his narrative: in fact it makes it considerably less plausible.

We are bound therefore to consider the third possibility: that Geoffrey made use of a source of information about the massacre that is no longer available to us. The only advantage of investigating this massacre so long after the event is that we are able to view it in a wider perspective; and out of this broad panorama of history there emerges a copycat massacre. In this later massacre, the Scots take the part of the Saxons, and the Picts of the Britons. The Scots, coming over in ever increasing numbers from Ireland, had gradually gained control of the Highlands of what is now Scotland, and the Picts were trying to maintain their hold on the rich agricultural areas to the east. A peace conference was convened and the leaders of the two sides accordingly met at Scone. The Scots, who were secretly armed, then set upon the Picts and murdered the king and all his nobles. From that date, about AD 850, the independent Pictish kingdoms ceased to exist and Kenneth MacAlpin, King of the Scots, became King of Scot-Land, a kingdom reaching from the Atlantic right across to the North Sea. The earliest authority for this story is Giraldus Cambrensis, writing about 350 years later.[8]

We now have two massacres recorded by three historians. The political and military settings for the massacres were very similar, as were the details of the massacres themselves. The essential elements are set out below in tabular form (with dates given in round figures, and Cloister of Ambrius abbreviated to C of A).

Date	Place	Winners	Losers	Historian
850	Scone	Scots	Picts	Giraldus
450	?	Saxons	Britons	Nennius
450	C of A	Saxons	Britons	Geoffrey

We have already seen that a massacre at the Cloister of Ambrius, on Salisbury Plain, seems incompatible with the historical setting in which it is placed. If two such massacres, seemingly quite unconnected, could take place, separated from one another by 400 years and as many miles, why not a third? This leads us to an interesting possibility which can be expressed in another table for comparison.

Date	Place	Winners	Losers	Historian
850	Scone	Scots	Picts	Giraldus
450	?	Saxons	Britons	Nennius
?	C of A	?	?	Geoffrey's source

If Geoffrey had heard a massacre story located at his Cloister of Ambrius, but did not know the date of the massacre nor the identity of the parties involved, what could be more natural than to slot the location of his massacre into the blank space in the *Kentish Chronicle* massacre and complete the picture?

There is of course a distinct possibility that these massacres have no more historical reality than the Grand old Duke of York's hill. They may, in other words, be no more than a convenient formula used by the losers for saying, in effect, 'It wasn't our fault we lost the war. It was the enemy. They cheated!' – much more satisfactory than having to face the possibility that their failure might have been due to their own incompetence. It matters very little whether the massacres themselves really happened or not. There can be no doubt about the political disasters that they represent. Gildas has nothing to say about the fifth-century massacre, but leaves us in no doubt about the extent of the disaster:

> All the major towns were laid low by the repeated battering of enemy rams; laid low too the inhabitants – church leaders, priests and people alike, as the swords glinted all around and the flames crackled. It was a sad sight. In the middle of the squares the foundation-stones of high walls and towers that had been torn from their lofty base, holy altars, fragments of corpses, covered (as it were) with a purple crust of congealed blood, looked as though they had been mixed up in some dreadful wine-press. There was no burial to be had except in the ruins of houses or the bellies of beasts and birds.[9]

The Cloister of Ambrius thus becomes the possible site for a massacre, or at least the focal point for a major disaster, which was probably quite unconnected with the history of the sixth century AD. Several authorities have suggested that the Cloister of Ambrius was in Amesbury,[10] but this cannot be so. The cloister is described as situated on Mount Ambrius, whereas Amesbury is situated in the valley of the river Avon. Furthermore, the victims of the massacre were buried in the cemetery beside the monastery, not two-and-a-half miles down the road from it. It is quite clear that, although there may have been some confusion in the mind of Geoffrey of Monmouth, the Cloister of Ambrius and Stonehenge are one and the same place.

The name 'Cloister of Ambrius' (*cenobium Ambrii*) is itself rather curi-ous. The Latin *cenobium* may be translated as 'cloister' in the usual sense of 'a covered arcade forming part of a religious or collegiate establish-ment',[11] a perfectly plausible description of Stonehenge; or it may be translated as 'monastery', which is also one of the subsidiary meanings of the English word, cloister. Stonehenge, while certainly never a monastery, might well have been the Temple of Ambrius. Geoffrey, in order to write it into his history of the fifth century, would have found it necessary to convert such a temple into a Christian establishment. For him, the distinction between the Christian Britons and the pagan Saxons was an important one.

The Saxons, as Geoffrey rightly tells us, gave Stonehenge the name by which we all know it today. To them it was a wonderful and mysterious ruin, and they called it *Stanheng* (*Stanenges, Stanhenges* and *Stanhenge* are other early forms), meaning either 'hinged stones' or 'hanging stones'.[12] The Britons, also viewing it as a mysterious ruin, called it the Giant's Ring or the Giant's Dance (*Chorea gigantum*). This is a name for a build-ing on such a scale, and so wonderful, that it must have been built by a forgotten race of giants. Here it belongs with a large class of natural fea-tures and prehistoric sites popularly known to this day as, for example, Giant's Castle, Giant's Causeway, Giant's Cave, Giant's Grave, Giant's House and Giant's Quoit. If Geoffrey had wanted to invent a story to bring Stonehenge into his history, the British name for it would have provided him with the ideal setting.

Geoffrey's history begins with the adventures of Brutus, a descendant of Aeneas, who, after much travelling and fighting, landed with a depleted band of followers at Totnes. They found Britain 'most attractive, because of the delightful situation of its various regions, its forests and the great number of its rivers, which teemed with fish; and it filled Brutus and his comrades with a great desire to live there'.[13] Furthermore, the whole island was uninhabited except for a few giants. Brutus and his companions soon divided up the land and settled down to live there. Corineus, whose share was called Cornwall after him, took great delight in wrestling with the giants, of whom there were far more in this area than anywhere else.

The obvious context for a fictitious story about the Giant's Ring would have been in this early part of the history. But Geoffrey totally ignores the connection with giants and, instead, begins his Stonehenge story with the massacre at the Cloister of Ambrius. If this is a genuine folk memory of a Temple of Ambrius, and the evidence certainly seems to point in that direction, then that memory reaches back for over two thousand years, to the time when Stonehenge was a functional building and not a mysterious ruin. The natural reaction to such a suggestion has been well expressed by J.S.P. Tatlock: 'Modern semi-scientific conjecture about the actual origin of Stonehenge has no bearing on Geoffrey's account, simply because there is no thinkable channel by which the pre-historic facts could have reached him.'[14] This, of course, is a statement of opinion, not an established fact.

We have travelled a long way from the 'Arthurian' or dark-age period of British history, and it is time to take stock of our progress. In the last chapter, it appeared that the Arthurian legend did not start with a military leader in the sixth century AD. By that time Arthur was a well-established legendary hero. In this chapter we have seen that Merlin, a well known legendary character in his own right and a generation senior to Arthur in Geoffrey's history, was closely connected with the building, of Stonehenge, a possible birthplace (or birth period) for the legends of both of them. In the absence of written records from prehistoric Britain, it would be impossible to corroborate such a legendary connection. But there is more to Geoffrey's story than this, and some of its other components may be more amenable to testing, for example by archaeological methods.

Stonehenge, or the Temple of Ambrius, was the site of a massacre or the focal point of a people who suffered a terrible, perhaps terminal, disaster. The stones were brought by sea from Ireland. Stonehenge was built as a memorial to the dead and was subsequently used as a burial place, particularly for the kings. These are all parts of Geoffrey's story about Stonehenge, and on such matters the archaeological record may provide crucial evidence.

CHAPTER 4

GREEK CONNECTION: THE HYPERBOREANS

For the pre-Roman history of Britain, the sources are limited. Diodorus Siculus, writing in the first century BC, gives a description based partly on the voyage of Pytheas of Massilia, who circumnavigated Britain about 300 BC.[1]

As for the inhabitants, they are simple and far removed from the shrewdness and vice which characterize our day. Their way of living is modest, since they are well clear of the luxury which is begotten of wealth. The island is also thickly populated and its climate is extremely cold, as one would expect, since it actually lies under the Great Bear. It is held by many kings and potentates, who for the most part live at peace among themselves.

This hardly seems the setting for the birth of a great legend, even though the inhabitants of Britain did have contact with the Mediterranean world through the export of tin from Cornwall. The tin was carried in cartloads at low tide to the island of *Ictis* (probably St Michael's Mount), and from there shipped across the sea to Gaul. The tin merchants then made their way across Gaul on foot, with the tin being transported on horseback, and eventually reached the mouth of the Rhone after a journey of about thirty days.

Diodorus also wrote about an island inhabited by the Hyperboreans, but felt that this might be more legendary than factual.[2]

Of those who have written about the ancient myths, Hecateus and certain others say that in the regions beyond the land of the Celts (Gaul) there lies in the ocean an island no smaller than Sicily. This island, the account continues, is situated in the north, and is inhabited by the Hyperboreans, who are called by that name because their home is beyond the point whence the north wind (Boreas) blows; and the land is both fertile and productive of every crop, and since it has an unusually temperate climate it produces two harvests each year.

The geographical setting leaves little room for doubt that this island of the Hyperboreans must also be Britain, though, from the contrasting descriptions it is little wonder that Diodorus failed to make the correlation.

The Hyperboreans also have a language, we are informed, which is peculiar to them, and are most friendly disposed towards the Greeks, and especially towards the Athenians and the Delians, who have inherited this goodwill from most ancient times. The myth also relates that certain Greeks visited the Hyperboreans and left behind them costly votive offerings bearing inscriptions in Greek letters. And in the same way Abaris, a Hyperborean, came to Greece in ancient times and renewed the goodwill and kinship of his people to the Delians.

Diodorus, in the first century BC, treats this material with caution, recognizing that much of it is of a legendary character. He also keeps reminding us that he is not writing from first-hand knowledge, by using such phrases as 'the account continues', 'we are informed' and 'the myth also relates'. The other point that is stressed is that these myths relate to ancient times, and that must mean ancient to Hecateus, writing about 500 BC, rather than ancient to Diodorus in the first century BC. Unfortunately, the writings of Hecateus have not survived. In the absence of Hecateus, we turn naturally to Herodotus, the father of history, who was writing in the fifth century BC, a generation or so later than Hecateus.

Herodotus has a good deal to say about the Hyperboreans and tells us quite clearly that his information comes from the Delians, the inhabitants of the little Aegean island of Delos.[3] He records how, in his own time:

Certain sacred offerings wrapped up in wheat straw come from the Hyperboreans into Scythia, whence they are taken over by the neighbouring peoples in succession until they get as far west as the Adriatic:

from there they are sent south, and the first Greeks to receive them are the Dodonaeans. Then, continuing southward, they reach the Malian gulf, cross to Euboea, and are passed on from town to town as far as Carystus. Then they skip Andros, the Carystians take them to Tenos, and the Tenians to Delos. That is how these things are said to reach Delos at the present time.

Herodotus goes on to put all this in its historical perspective. When these offerings were first brought to Delos, they were carried by two girls, Hyperoche and Laodice, who were escorted by five men. But they stayed in Delos and died there. So when the Hyperboreans found that their messengers did not return they adopted the practice of 'wrapping the offerings in straw and taking them to the border, with instructions to their neighbours to see them conveyed to their destination by a process of relay, from one nation to another'. The tomb of Hyperoche and Laodice was situated by the entrance to the temple of Artemis, on the left as you go in, and had an olive tree growing on it. In the time of Herodotus it was the custom of girls, before they were married, to cut off a lock of their hair, wrap it round a spindle, and place it on the tomb in memory of the two Hyperborean girls. Even earlier, two other Hyperborean girls, Arge and Opis, had come to Delos and stayed there. Their tomb stands behind the temple of Artemis and faces towards the east. Arge and Opis came to Delos at the same time as Apollo and Artemis 'and are therefore honoured in a different way; for the women of Delos make collections for them, and name them in the hymn which Olen of Lycea wrote in their honour'.

The tenuous connection between the Hyperboreans and the Delians, which was still maintained in the fifth century BC, was not only of great antiquity, but also seems rather less mythical than Diodorus would have us believe. Herodotus even hints that it began at the same time as the worship of Apollo and Artemis was introduced to Delos. This is in complete accord with what Diodorus has to say about the Hyperboreans and their island. He tells us that Leto, the mother of Apollo, was born on this island, and 'for that reason Apollo is honoured among them above all other gods; and the inhabitants are looked upon as priests of Apollo, after a manner, since daily they praise this god continuously in song and honour him exceedingly'.

Herodotus mentions references to the Hyperboreans in the works of

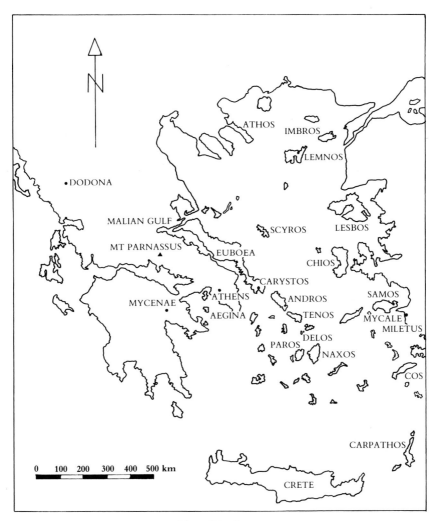

Map of the Aegean

Hesiod and Homer. Homer, writing in the eighth century BC, makes a passing reference to them, as a distant people, in his Hymn to Dionysus,[4] but his greatest contribution to this story is in the wonderful Hymn to Delian Apollo.[5] This tells the story of how Leto came to give birth to Apollo on Mount Cynthus, on the little rocky island of Delos. She had been to Crete and Athens, and to the islands of Aegina, Euboea, Athos, Samos, Scyros, Imbros, Lemnos, Lesbos, Chios, Mycale, Cos, Carpathos, Naxos and Paros, as well as some cities on the mainland, such as Miletus. The list reads like a comprehensive tour of the Aegean. 'So far roamed Leto in travail . . . to see if any would be willing to make a dwelling for her son. But they greatly trembled and feared and none, not even the richest of them dared receive Phoebus [Apollo], until queenly Leto set foot on Delos.'

Then Leto promised Delos that though her soil was poor, if she would make a home for her son Phoebus Apollo and build a great temple for him, pilgrims would come from far and wide. 'And you will feed those that dwell in you from the hand of strangers', said Leto. Delos was not easily persuaded, and greatly feared that when Apollo saw the light of day he would scorn the little island, with its hard rocky soil, and would trample it down into the depths of the sea. Then Leto swore the great oath of the gods, that her son should have his temple and that he should honour Delos above all others. Delos was finally convinced and, after nine days of painful labour, Leto gave birth to Apollo. The hymn ends: 'I will never cease to praise far-shooting Apollo, god of the silver bow, whom rich-haired Leto bare.'

This is as far as we can go with the written word and here we are truly in the misty borderland between history and legend. Homer's great epics of the Heroic Age of Greece were widely believed to be myths until, a little over a century ago, Heinrich Schliemann made his famous discovery of Troy and began his excavations there. The events recorded in the *Iliad* and the *Odyssey* took place some five hundred years before Homer's time, but were of such importance and interest that they had been passed down in verse and song, from generation to generation through the centuries, and remembered. If anyone doubts the reality of the events described by Homer, they should read Tim Severin's graphic account of his own epic voyage in a 'Bronze Age' galley, in which he followed the route taken by Odysseus (Ulysses) on his return from Troy.[6]

Even the more unlikely adventures which befell Odysseus turned out to be very real, when the journey was made the way Odysseus himself made it.

What we have to do now is to extract the likely historical content from the writings of Diodorus, Herodotus and Homer, and see what they can tell us about the Hyperboreans. There seems to have been regular contact between the Hyperboreans and the Greeks over many centuries, and this began when the Hyperboreans introduced the Greeks to the worship of Apollo. This is quite contrary to the old view that the culture flow was all in one direction, from the Mediterranean civilizations outwards to the relatively barbarous peoples of the north and west. Furthermore, this contact must have been initiated sometime before about 1250 BC the approximate date of the Trojan war, by which time the worship of Apollo was well established.

These Hyperboreans, appearing as they do in the legends of far-off Greece, seem a much more likely starting point for our native Arthurian legends than the relatively impoverished inhabitants of Britain in the time of Pytheas. They were people of some standing, not only locally but also, like Arthur himself, on the wider international scene. An important feature of this historical summary is that, like some of Geoffrey of Monmouth's statements about Stonehenge, it can be tested against the archaeological record.

Before we take leave of the historical sources, Diodorus has one more thing to tell us about the Hyperboreans, which has received a great deal of publicity in recent years and is fundamental to our own investigation.

And there is also on the island both a magnificent sacred precinct of Apollo and a notable temple which is adorned with many votive offerings and is spherical in shape. Furthermore, a city is there which is sacred to this god, and the majority of its inhabitants are players on the cithara; and these continually play on this instrument in the temple and sing hymns of praise to the god, glorifying his deeds . . . They say also that the moon, as viewed from this island, appears to be but a little distance from the earth and to have upon it prominences, like those of the earth, which are visible to the eye. The account is also given that the god visits the island every nineteen years, the period in which the return of the stars to the same place in the heavens is accomplished, and for this reason the nineteen year period is called by the Greeks the 'year of Meton'.[7] At the time of this appearance of the god he both plays on the cithara and dances continuously the night through from the vernal equinox until the rising of the Pleiades, expressing in this manner his delight in his successes. And the kings of this city and the supervisors of the sacred precinct are called Boreades, since they are descendants of Boreas, and the succession to these positions is always kept in their family.

A spherical temple sounds a rather unlikely structure but Stonehenge seems to fit the description better than any other site, and this correlation has been very widely accepted. When complete, the most remarkable feature of Stonehenge was the circle of sarsen standing stones capped with a continuous ring of lintels, so beautifully constructed that the joints between them were hardly visible and their surface was almost exactly horizontal. When standing inside this circle, the surrounding landscape was almost totally obscured by the massive stone uprights, and the ring of lintel stones provided an artificial horizon, above which the sky extended uninterrupted, like a great inverted hemispherical bowl. Viewing the stars at night, it was abundantly clear that this hemisphere was just one half of the complete sphere of the heavens which, studded with innumerable stars, was continuously revolving around the earth. A temple with the unique design of Stonehenge was as nearly spherical as it was possible to be.

If the island of the Hyperboreans really was Britain and the spherical temple Stonehenge, and there seems every reason to accept this correlation, then Diodorus has led us to exactly the same period in prehistory as was indicated, over a thousand years later, by Geoffrey of Monmouth. In this context, it seems to have escaped notice that the passage quoted above contains internal dating evidence. The statement that the god danced through the night, from the vernal equinox to the rising of the Pleiades, seems to imply that the rising of the Pleiades would have provided a signal for the dancing to stop. This would make no sense at all at the present time, because at the vernal equinox the Pleiades rise about two hours after the sun and could not possibly be observed. Further-more, the rising of the Pleiades is, in any case, a slightly unreal concept. The stars in this well-known cluster are individually so faint that they would not be visible until they had risen well above the horizon.

The dating evidence inherent in the statement that the god danced through the night, from the vernal equinox to the rising of the Pleiades, depends on the precession of the equinoxes. Over a period of 26,000 years, the equinoxes move through all the constellations of the zodiac and back to their starting point. At the present time the vernal equinox is in the constellation of Pisces, which means that the sun is in Pisces around 21 March. Between 2,000 and 4,000 years ago, the vernal equinox would have been in Aries, and before that in Taurus, the constellation containing the Pleiades. About 2000 BC, the Pleiades would have risen at the same time as the sun at the vernal equinox. It would of course have been much too close to the sun to be visible but, to an observer familiar with the night sky, its position could have been determined from familiar bright stars (for example in Cassiopeia and Perseus) above it.

A date of around 2000 BC for the nineteen-yearly returns and equinoctial dances of the god is consistent with the date of some time before 1250 BC, derived from the Greek–Hyperborean–Apollo link. The two dates, though ultimately based on the same source, are in fact totally independent, one being based on astronomical analysis and the other on historical analysis. Their consistency is a good reason for believing that our sources contain much more genuine historical material than might otherwise have been supposed. Furthermore, it will not have escaped notice that, while the prehistoric Hyperborean culture was centred on its spherical temple (Stonehenge), the Arthur–Merlin legend was centred on the Temple of Ambrius (Stonehenge). The historical sources are converging to direct our attention to a single place and time for a Heroic Age in prehistoric Britain.

PART II

TESTING THE HISTORICAL SOURCES

CHAPTER 5

STONEHENGE: SOME LEGENDS TESTED

Stonehenge, to which the historical sources have directed us, is one of the wonders of Britain. Henry of Huntingdon, writing about 1130, was the first whose thoughts on Stonehenge as an ancient monument have come down to us.

> Stanenges, where stones of wonderful size have been erected after the manner of doorways, so that doorway appears to have been raised upon doorway, and no one can conceive how such great stones have been raised aloft, or why they were built there.

This is the first item in the rich and varied literature on Stonehenge, assembled and reviewed by Christopher Chippindale in his book *Stonehenge Complete*.[1] The best account of Stonehenge itself is still Professor Atkinson's book *Stonehenge*,[2] first published in 1956; while Julian Richards, in a recent book also entitled *Stonehenge*,[3] sets the site in its prehistoric environment, as revealed by the latest excavations and surveys.

The long history of Stonehenge began with the construction of an earthwork: a circular bank of chalk with a single opening to the north-east. The material for the bank was dug from a discontinuous external quarry ditch. Just inside the bank was a circle of fifty-six pits, back-filled soon after they were dug, and known as the Aubrey Holes, after their seventeenth-century discoverer, John Aubrey. Whatever other use Stonehenge I may have had, it certainly served as a cemetery right from

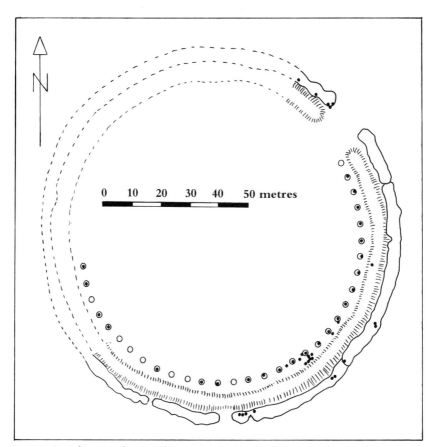

Stonehenge I, showing the excavated portions of the bank and ditch, the
excavated Aubrey Holes (open circles) and the Neolithic cremations
(black dots)

the beginning. Of the thirty-four Aubrey Holes which have been excavated, twenty-five contained deposits of cremated bones, buried in the
chalk filling. Similar cremation burials were found in the ditch (one right
at the bottom), in the bank, and just inside the bank. None were found
in the area enclosed by the Aubrey Hole circle, in spite of extensive and
careful excavation. Some of the Aubrey Hole cremations are accompanied by a limited supply of grave goods, particularly flint 'fabricators'
and bone pins, indicating a general later-Neolithic date. Radiocarbon

Oblique aerial view of Stonehenge from the south-east

dates from three antler picks, used in digging the quarry ditch and abandoned there, give a date of about 3000 BC.[4]

Stonehenge II, of which no trace remains above the ground, consisted of an incomplete double circle of bluestones, dark-coloured igneous rocks foreign to Salisbury Plain, with extra stones flanking an entrance to the north-east. The existence of these former standing stones was revealed during Atkinson's excavations in the 1950s. Radially arranged pairs of stone holes (the Q and R holes), filled with tightly rammed chalk rubble, were found either side of the surviving bluestone circle. Their function was indicated by the crushed surface of the chalk at the bottom of the holes and associated splinters of bluestone. Apart from the fact that the Q and R holes are structurally older than the existing circles of Stonehenge III, there is little direct evidence for dating Stonehenge II. An antler pick from the bottom of an unfinished R hole gave a radiocarbon date of about 2100 BC for the end of Period II. By that time, the construction of Stonehenge I was as long ago to them as the Norman Conquest is to us.

If Stonehenge II was planned as a double stone circle which, when completed, would serve some religious or other public function, then it must be considered a colossal administrative blunder. By the time the project was abandoned, the labour force had already dragged some fifty stones to the site, each weighing several tons, and set them up in their places. Are we really to believe that at this point the management suddenly decided that there was a serious design fault, and that they would have to dismantle the whole thing and start all over again with much larger stones of a different sort?

It seems much more likely that these stones were erected individually over a long period of time, like the stones in a modern graveyard, but, unlike gravestones, set up in an ordered pattern in the sacred enclosure rather than by the grave itself. It will be recalled that Geoffrey of Monmouth said that the stones were placed there as a memorial to the dead. Before this is dismissed as wishful speculation, there are a few other pieces of evidence to be considered.

Outside Stonehenge, the earliest archaeological site in the area containing a bluestone is Boles Barrow, a Neolithic long barrow situated about twelve miles west of Stonehenge. Boles Barrow was excavated by William Cunnington in 1801 and, unlike most of the long barrows on Salisbury Plain, turned out to be a cairn of loosely piled rocks, so loose indeed that they came tumbling down during the excavation, and brought the work to a halt. Most of the rocks were sarsen stones of local origin, but with these was a single boulder of bluestone weighing several hundred pounds.[5] Boles Barrow is not itself dated, but seems to belong to a burial tradition probably rather earlier than the Stonehenge I cemetery.

The association of bluestones with burials continues into the Bronze Age, in the round barrows around Stonehenge. Many of these round barrows were also excavated by Cunnington in the early nineteenth century and others by Stukeley in the eighteenth century. Some of them contained fresh chips of bluestone, apparently deposited as part of the grave goods. These chips, unlike the boulder in Boles Barrow, were probably removed from the stones at Stonehenge, some perhaps legitimately and others possibly by stealth. In this connection, a burial in the Stonehenge ditch is of particular interest. The burial was discovered during a small-scale excavation in 1978, north-west of the entrance. The buried man had been shot at close range by three arrows tipped with barbed and tanged flint arrowheads. This type of arrowhead is broadly contemporary with many of the round barrows in the vicinity of Stonehenge. The grave also contained fragments of bluestone. A likely explanation is that the man had been caught in the act of removing pieces of bluestone from Stonehenge, and was summarily executed for his crime.

The only part of Stonehenge containing a continuous record from the very beginning is the ditch. This was about 2 m (7 ft) deep at its deepest and, during the course of its 5,000-year history, accumulated about 1.8 m (6 ft) of deposits, leaving only a shallow depression to mark its position at the present time. The sediments in the ditch can be divided into three broad categories: the early coarse chalk silt, 0.9 m (3 ft) thick; the later fine chalk silt, 0.45 m (1.5 ft) thick; and the earthy soil, 0.45 m (1.5 ft) thick. The early coarse silt accumulated rapidly, while the sides of the ditch were still steep and fresh, and the adjacent bank was not protected from erosion by a cover of turf. The later fine, chalky silt accumulated more slowly, as the ditch assumed a gentler, more stable profile and the sides were protected by a cover of vegetation. The overlying soil accumulated more slowly still. The burial mentioned above, radiocarbon dated to about 2200 BC, was dug into the fine chalky silt layer. A few fragments of bluestone have been found near the bottom of this same chalky silt. These fragments must have found their way into the ditch (how or why we do not know) centuries before 2200 BC; and the first bluestones may have been on the site for an unknown period of time before these particular pieces were deposited in the ditch. The implication of the ditch sequence is quite unequivocal. The bluestones were being brought to Stonehenge over a period of hundreds of years, before Stonehenge II was finally abandoned. This, together with the Neolithic and Bronze Age burial associations, is consistent with the idea that the stones, which once stood in the Q and R holes, were individual memo-rials to the dead rather than components of a planned double stone circle which was never completed.

Period III began with the building of the most magnificent example of prehistoric architecture in the whole of Britain: the lintelled circle of sarsen stones and the horseshoe (U-shaped) setting of gigantic sarsen stone trilithons (two uprights and a lintel across the top).

The sarsen circle, when complete, consisted of thirty standing stones surmounted by a continuous ring of lintel stones. It is the most accurately constructed of all the British stone circles. The stones, all of which have been dressed to shape, have their inner faces tangent to a circle 29.642 m (97.25 ft) in diameter, with a mean error of about 7.5 cm (3 in). With each upright weighing about twenty-six tons, this is an astonishing feat of prehistoric engineering. The upper surface of this lintelled circle, horizontal and level at a height of 4.9 m (16 ft) above the ground, was wide enough for two people to walk on it side by side. The most beautiful feature of this building is the way that the inner and outer faces of the individual lintel stones have been shaped to form arcs of the circle on which they lie. This is a true circle, rather than a roughly circular polygon.

The stones are joined to one another in a manner generally associated with timber structures. The lintels are fixed to the uprights by means of mortice and tenon joints. Each upright has a pair of protuberances (tenons) on top, which fitted into corresponding hollows (mortice holes) in the lintels above. Furthermore, the lintels are joined to one another by tongue and groove joints.

The sarsen trilithons are like huge detached sections of the sarsen

Part of the sarsen circle of Stonehenge showing the curvature of the lintels. Four stones of the bluestone circle (two standing and two fallen) can also be seen

circle. As in the sarsen circle, the inner and outer faces of the lintels are curved to fit the shape of which they form a part. The trilithons are considerably taller than the sarsen circle, and their heights are graded, with the tallest being at the south-western, closed end of the horseshoe. The top of this great trilithon formerly stood at a height of 7.3 m (24 ft) above ground level, towering 2.4 m (8 ft) above the sarsen circle.

The lintel stones of the trilithons are carefully shaped, not only in the curvature of their inner and outer faces, but also in cross-section. Unlike those of the circle, they are not rectangular but are 15 cm (6 in) wider at the top than at the bottom. This must have been designed to counteract the effect of perspective, which, at that height, would have given the lintels the appearance of tapering upwards. Such a device was not needed on the circle because, when complete, none of the lintels would have been visible end on.

Here, if anywhere, is the spherical temple so admired by the ancient Greeks of Delos. Its date is therefore of considerable importance. A discarded antler pick in the packing of the ramp leading down to one of the sarsen stones gave a date of about 2200 BC. Two antler picks from the Avenue ditches, extending north-eastwards from the entrance, gave similar dates, indicating structural activity outside, as well as inside the enclosure at this time. At this date, the God would have had no problem dancing through the night from the vernal equinox to the rising of the Pleiades. The Pleiades, rising perhaps a little before the sun, would not have been visible but could have been located, as explained in the last chapter, by reference to familiar brighter stars in the sky above. The archaeological evidence at Stonehenge is in complete accord with the dating unknowingly supplied by Diodorus Siculus.

After the building of Stonehenge IIIa was complete, work started on the displaced bluestones. The architect had clearly planned something (Stonehenge IIIb) in keeping with the sarsen building described above. Stones were shaped, tenons sculpted, and mortice holes hollowed out. The plan involved the erection of at least two trilithons, and also involved two stones quite unlike anything in Stonehenge IIIa. One of these has a long groove running down one side for its full height. The other, a stump revealed by excavation, has a corresponding ridge or tongue down what is left of its height. Though not now adjacent, these two stones look as if they had been intended as a pair, joined along their full height by a tongue and groove joint, a device known in timber work

Grooved bluestone, with the second sarsen trilithon in the background

as matchboarding. Whatever was on the drawing board or in the architect's mind, it was certainly not the bluestone setting whose meagre remains (Stonehenge IIIc) we see today. This consists of a circle and horseshoe of bluestone uprights with, so far as possible, all trace of the planned structure removed – tenons hammered away almost beyond recognition, mortice holes and the tongue and groove of the matchboarded pair facing away from the centre.

Following Atkinson, it has generally been assumed that Stonehenge IIIb (or at least that part of it involving carefully shaped stones) actually existed, either at Stonehenge or nearby, and was subsequently dismantled. But why destroy a building which, to judge from the quality of the surviving stonework, must have been of great beauty? What was the function of the matchboarded pair of stones? Joining two stones together so that they look like one seems a completely pointless exercise. It would make more sense if a number of stones had been joined in this way, perhaps to form a secure chamber, a place maybe where the religious treasures of Stonehenge might have been kept. If that were so, these two stones would be the sole record of an architectural innovation which never got beyond the pilot stage of development.

It is more likely that the stones were still being prepared for Stonehenge IIIb when the architect died, leaving no one capable of putting his plans into effect. Unable to follow the original design, they could not afford to ignore such important and historic stones. The best they could manage was a feeble imitation of the master's work: a circle and horseshoe of standing stones in the shadow of the massive lintelled sarsen structures. By turning the mortice holes and grooved stone to face the wall, so to speak (the tongue may have been hammered away down to ground level) and removing the tenons, they may have been trying to give the impression that Stonehenge IIIb had never even been thought of, rather than admit that they had failed to bring it to completion. Alternatively there may have been a superstitious feeling that the ancient memorial stones had somehow been desecrated; that the great architect had gone too far in trying to incorporate them into his architectural scheme. Whatever the story that lies behind them, the bluestone circle and horseshoe represent the final stage of building work at Stonehenge. There is no direct dating evidence, but it seems likely that little time was involved in the various developments of Stonehenge III.

How does the Stonehenge of archaeology fit with the Cloister of
Ambrius and Stonehenge of Geoffrey of Monmouth, and the spherical
temple of Diodorus? It is time to take stock of the evidence.

In its earliest phase, the central area of Stonehenge was surrounded by
its own cemetery, in the Aubrey Holes and the bank and ditch. Later on
it was the centre for the greatest assemblage of round barrows anywhere
in the country, some of them rich enough to be considered the burials
of kings. Geoffrey had his kings buried within the circle of stones,
which is certainly not true at Stonehenge, but this can be interpreted as
'medievalizing' the record to bring it into line with contemporary custom. In Geoffrey's time, the kings were buried *inside* the great cathedrals

Stonehenge, at the centre of the greatest concentration
of Bronze Age round barrows in Britain

and abbey churches. The bluestones of the second period may well have been erected as memorials to the dead, as recorded by Geoffrey. For Diodorus, the dating of Stonehenge III is the most important piece of evidence. As far as it goes, the archaeological evidence is in good agreement with the historical record discussed in earlier chapters. The one thing missing is the disaster, which plays such an important part in Geoffrey's history as the massacre at the Cloister of Ambrius. The supposed death of the great architect, considered above, was a personal rather than a national disaster, and would hardly satisfy the legend.

Apart from a few outlying sarsen stones (the Heel Stone, the Slaughter Stone, the Station Stones) and some associated ring ditches and stone holes, which have no bearing on the present investigation, there is just one feature of Stonehenge remaining to be considered. This is a double circle of pits, outside the sarsen stone circle, known as the Y and Z holes. They are structurally later than the sarsen circle, but have no contact with any of the bluestones. They therefore belong either to one of the later phases of Stonehenge III or to some entirely separate later phase. Atkinson thought that they had probably been intended as stone holes for the unworked bluestones of Stonehenge IIIb, though it was clear from their excavation that they never actually held stones. Something went wrong before the work was completed. All trace of the planned structure was, as far as possible, removed from sight, and the bluestones were set up as we see them today. As far as the Y and Z holes are concerned, there is one fundamental flaw in this explanation. The holes were left open: an eyesore, a hazard for the unwary visitor and a glaring reminder of a design that was never completed.

Were the Y and Z holes ever even intended as stone holes? The evidence seems to suggest otherwise. A stone hole must be appreciably larger than the stone it is to house. When the stone is set up in the hole, the space around it must be filled and packed tight in order to make the stone stable. The most convenient source of packing material would be the spoil from digging the holes, which was therefore usually piled up nearby. There is no evidence for the presence or former existence of such heaps of chalk adjacent to the Y and Z holes. Had there been such heaps, the chalk from them would have washed back into the pits as a layer of coarse chalk rubble, like the early silting in the ditch. Instead, apart from a thin basal layer of chalk rubble, such as might be derived

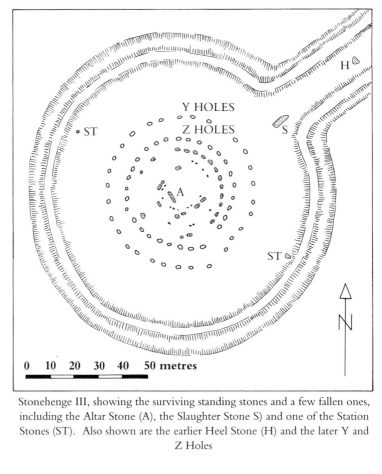

Stonehenge III, showing the surviving standing stones and a few fallen ones, including the Altar Stone (A), the Slaughter Stone S) and one of the Station Stones (ST). Also shown are the earlier Heel Stone (H) and the later Y and Z Holes

from the walls of the pits themselves, their filling was composed of fine brown soil. The evidence of this filling suggests that they were dug as pits, and intended from the outset to be left open as pits.

If the Y and Z holes were not stone holes and were not part of the great Stonehenge IIIb plan, they are likely to represent something entirely separate. They are totally out of character with the rest of the structures in the central area. Open pits are the absolute antithesis of standing stones, reaching downwards into the depths of the earth instead of upwards towards the heavens above. Whatever a double circle of stones may have stood for, a double circle of pits must have represented the exact opposite. The Y and Z holes represent the most fundamental change in the whole long history of Stonehenge.

The only link between the Y and Z holes and the bluestones consists of one or two fresh chips of bluestone deposited at the bottom of each hole. There can be no reasonable doubt that these pieces of bluestone were deposited intentionally, though why they were so deposited is much less easy to determine. On Atkinson's hypothesis, they were symbolic offerings, in place of the stones that should have occupied the holes. On the hypothesis outlined above, they would represent a ritual slighting of the standing stones, followed by a token gesture of returning them to the depths whence they came: a negation of their former function of reaching for the sky.

An antler pick from one of the Y holes gave a radiocarbon date of about 1550 BC, centuries after the likely completion of Stonehenge III. From this date, Stonehenge ceased to be a functional building and gradually fell into decay, a decay accelerated much later on by intentional demolition. Radiocarbon dates of about 1350 BC and 1000 BC, from the curved eastward extension of the avenue, near Amesbury, are not matched by any activity at Stonehenge itself, and this extension to the avenue was probably intended to serve as a territorial boundary. The history of Stonehenge ends abruptly with the digging of the Y and Z holes.

The date of about 1550 BC for the end of Stonehenge is also a significant date in the surrounding country. It marks the end of the great Wessex Culture, notable for some of the richest prehistoric graves in Britain. The enormity of the cultural break at this time was well expressed some years ago by Burgess:

> The passing of the Wessex culture graphically illustrates the magnitude of this hiatus . . . . Its end could not . . . have been long and lingering, but what, apart from some catastrophe, could have induced it so rapidly, and could have brought comparable changes not only throughout Britain and Ireland, but even across the Channel in Brittany? The pattern hardly suggests natural change, nor is there any evidence of invasions or migrations. It is difficult to think of any other human force which could have been more than contributory.[6]

If Geoffrey of Monmouth's massacre at the Cloister of Ambrius is to be interpreted as a prehistoric disaster on a national scale, here we have it. The end of Stonehenge was the end of an era.

CHAPTER 6

STONES FROM IRELAND: MERLIN TESTED

Geoffrey of Monmouth tells us that, when Merlin suggested to Aurelius that he should send an expedition to Ireland to collect the stones from the Giant's Ring on Mount Killaraus, the King burst out laughing:

'How can such large stones be moved from so far-distant a country?' he asked. 'It is hardly as if Britain itself is lacking in stones big enough for the job!' 'Try not to laugh in a foolish way, your Majesty,' answered Merlin. 'What I am suggesting has nothing ludicrous about it. These stones are connected with certain secret religious rites and they have various properties which are medicinally important. Many years ago the Giants transported them from the remotest confines of Africa and set them up in Ireland at a time when they inhabited that country. Their plan was that, whenever they felt ill, baths should be prepared at the foot of the stones; for they used to pour water over them and to run this water into baths in which their sick were cured. What is more, they mixed the water with herbal concoctions and so healed their wounds. There is not a single stone among them which hasn't some medicinal value.'[1]

The King's reaction to Merlin's suggestion that the stones should be imported from overseas is completely unmedieval. In Geoffrey's own time, importing the stone for great building works was common practice. Canterbury Cathedral was built of stone shipped over from Caen, in Normandy, and the same stone was used at Rochester, St Albans and Winchester. This story looks like a pre-medieval tradition; a tradition dating back to a time when shipping stones across the sea would truly have been something to marvel at. And choosing stones for a memorial to the Christian victims of a pagan massacre, because they were associated with secret religious rites and had mysterious healing powers, seems hardly appropriate, even for the sixth-century setting in which Geoffrey placed the story.

The stones of Stonehenge have for centuries been recognized as belonging to two distinct rock types, known as the sarsen stones and the bluestones. The sarsen stones are a very hard type of sandstone, in which the quartz grains are cemented together by a secondary deposit of crystalline quartz. Their local origin has long been recognized, and large blocks of sarsen stone, known as grey wethers, can still be seen lying on the surface on the Marlborough Downs. The bluestones, with the exception of the so-called Altar Stone, are all igneous rocks and quite foreign to the Salisbury Plain area. The possibility of testing Geoffrey of Monmouth's story, therefore, lies with these bluestones.

Locating the source of building stones depends on three vital factors: (i) a good knowledge of the petrology of the stones concerned, (ii) good geological maps and a corresponding knowledge of the rocks in the possible source areas, and (iii) an element of luck; and let no one underestimate the importance of luck. All too often, such stones turn out to be of so widespread a rock type that there is no possibility of pinpointing their source without documentary or other supporting evidence.

For the Stonehenge bluestones, all these ingredients for a successful interpretation came together when H.H. Thomas, an officer of the Geological Survey, first visited the site in 1920. Thomas had been consulted about the petrology of some bluestone chips from Stonehenge as early as 1906, but had been unable to reach any firm conclusions. In the intervening years he had been engaged in the geological mapping of south Pembrokeshire (Dyfed). During the course of this work, he began to notice glacial boulders of dolerite with highly distinctive white spots. So remarkable were these boulders, that Thomas and his colleagues marked them individually on their maps. When their distribution was examined, it was found to be elongated, with an axis pointing north-westwards directly towards Mynydd Preselau (sometimes referred to as the Prescelly or Preseli Mountains), beyond the limits of the region they were mapping at the time. A subsequent visit to Mynydd Preselau revealed spotted dolerite *in situ* and confirmed the suspected source for the boulders. When at length Thomas visited Stonehenge, he realized at once that many of the bluestones were none other than these familiar and highly distinctive spotted dolerites of Pembrokeshire. He had arrived at Stonehenge armed with the one vital clue to the mystery of the bluestones.

The spotted dolerites were not the only rock type represented among the bluestones, but they were the most abundant and also, by good fortune, the most distinctive. The other bluestones included unspotted dolerite, flow banded rhyolite (a type of volcanic rock) and an altered volcanic ash. Before completing his research, Thomas made a microscopic examination of thin sections, taken from the different sorts of Stonehenge bluestone, and compared them with thin sections of similar rocks from all over the country, in the extensive Geological Survey collections. The spotted dolerites, which have since become known as preselite, are a very local variety of a group of igneous rocks intruded into the Lower Ordovician volcanic rocks of Pembrokeshire (Dyfed). These volcanic rocks include flow banded rhyolites and altered volcanic ashes identical with those found at Stonehenge. On the slopes of Mynydd Preselau, particularly in the immediate vicinity of Carn Meini and Carn Alw, there are vast accumulations of boulders, dolerite, rhyolite and other local rocks, torn from the frost-shattered peaks above. Further south, the glacial deposits also contain erratic boulders derived from more distant sources.

Thomas had demonstrated, once and for all, that Mynydd Preselau was the source of the igneous bluestones of Stonehenge. There was no longer the slightest possibility that they had, as in Geoffrey's history, been brought over from Ireland. Mynydd Preselau could, however, reasonably be described as being in a far distant country and, as Atkinson showed many years ago, it is most likely that the stones were transported (coastwise) by sea. Over the centuries, a journey round the Bristol Channel could easily have become 'a journey across the sea' and that, in turn, could equally easily have become a journey 'across the sea from Ireland'.

The Altar Stone, unlike all the other bluestones, quite certainly did not come from Mynydd Preselau. It is a micaceous sandstone, a very common and widespread rock type. By its colour and slightly calcareous cement, it seemed most likely to have come from the Old Red Sandstone of South Wales, either the Senni Beds which outcrop in a broad east-west belt right across Glamorganshire, or the Cosheston Group which occurs along the northern shores of Milford Haven in

Pembrokeshire. Detailed examination of its mineralogy suggested that the Altar Stone most probably came from the Cosheston Group, and therefore from somewhere in the Milford Haven area.

H.H. Thomas's report to the Society of Antiquaries in 1923 is the classic example of the application of petrology to an archaeological problem.[2] Not only did he successfully locate the ultimate geological source of the stones in question, but he then proceeded to tackle the difficult problem of how they were moved, whether by glacial action or by man. Professor Judd had already suggested that the bluestones were glacial erratics, so the conclusion that the builders of Stonehenge brought them all the way from Mynydd Preselau was by no means automatic.

If an ice sheet had in fact transported the bluestones to Salisbury Plain, it should have left substantial deposits of glacial drift. There are none. It should also have left glacial erratics, other than those found at Stonehenge. There are none: neither boulders nor pebbles in the local river gravels. Furthermore the known glacial deposits containing Pembrokeshire boulders indicate that the ice-front lay only just south of the present coastline of Pembrokeshire. Thomas concluded that:

> Such a hypothetical ice sheet, in order to account for the foreign stones of Stonehenge would have to gather from Pembrokeshire blocks all of about the same size and mainly of two rock types. It would have to carry them all that distance without dropping any by the way. Further, it would have to pass over all kinds of rocky obstacles without gathering to itself any of the various materials over which it was forced to ride. Such in itself, without the additional positive evidence that is forthcoming as to the extent of the glaciation of Pembrokeshire and adjoining counties, permanently disposes of the idea of glacial transport for the foreign stones of Stonehenge.

Convincing though that may have seemed at the time, the idea of glacial transport was not disposed of permanently. It was revived in 1971 by another officer of the Geological Survey, G.A. Kellaway.[3] Kellaway cited new evidence of glacial deposits in Somerset, some of them along the route that an ice sheet might have taken from Pembrokeshire to Salisbury Plain. At Holwell, near Nunney in the eastern Mendips, he found a deposit of red-brown clay containing fragments of chalk, flint, chert, sandstone, quartzite, and Carboniferous and Jurassic limestones. At Kenn, near Clevedon, north of the Mendips, a similar deposit contained flint, chert and rocks from the South Wales coalfield. Further south, around Westonzoyland, east of the Quantock Hills, deposits of glacial sand and gravel contain pebbles of Devonian, Carboniferous, Triassic, Jurassic and Cretaceous rocks, mostly originating in west Somerset and north Devon. Finally, in the storm beaches on the north side of Flat Holme, a small island in the Bristol Channel, between Cardiff and Weston-Super-Mare, pebbles of flint, chert, Old Red Sandstone, and a wide range of igneous rocks, from South Wales, North Wales and the Lake District, are found among the predominant local Carboniferous Limestone pebbles.

The evidence indicates that an ice sheet moved up the Bristol Channel from west to east and penetrated inland across parts of Somerset. There is, however, no evidence of any glacial deposits on Salisbury Plain and the deposits in Somerset are thin and carry no large boulders. A possible large erratic boulder at Westonzoyland, a rock known locally as the Devil's Upping Stock, had been cut up for ornamental stone some time earlier and its petrology was therefore unknown. In short, the glacial deposits of Somerset gave little reason for revising the conclusions of H.H. Thomas regarding the glacial origin of the Stonehenge bluestones.

If the bluestones of Stonehenge were glacial erratics, then other boulders of similar general character ought to be found in the neighbourhood. Only two such rocks are known and both are spotted dolerite. One is the rock found by Cunnington in Boles Barrow. The other is from Lake, in the Avon valley, just south of Amesbury. Where are all the other bluestone erratics? Surely the ice sheet did not transport the eighty or so stones required for Stonehenge and no more! To suggest, as Kellaway seems to imply, that there might be 5,000 tons of medium to large erratics hidden away in unexcavated long barrows on Salisbury Plain is surely clutching at archaeological straws. The almost total lack of bluestones on Salisbury Plain outside Stonehenge itself is a serious obstacle to the glacial theory of their transport.

If we consider the bluestones (the Stonehenge ones and the others) simply as an assemblage of different rock types, the most striking feature of this assemblage is that three quarters of them belong to a single rock type

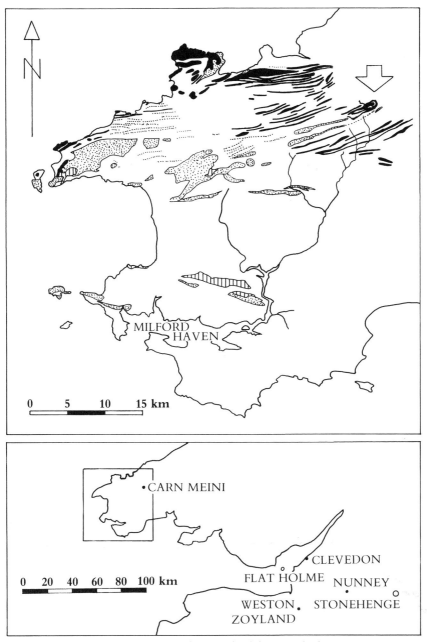

Map of south-west Britain, showing the dolerites and other intrusive
igneous rocks (black) and the volcanic rocks (stippled) of Pembrokeshire,
with the area occupied by the spotted dolerites of Mynydd Preselau circled

(spotted dolerite) and that this originated in a very restricted area on Mynydd Preselau. An ice sheet crossing Pembrokeshire would pass over extensive outcrops of potential bluestones. Among these, unspotted dolerites are far more widespread than the spotted variety. Volcanic rocks of various sorts are also far more abundant than spotted dolerites. And, in the west, there are outcrops of granodiorite at least as extensive as the spotted dolerites in the east. The ratios of igneous rock types among the bluestones are thus quite incompatible with glacial transport from Pembrokeshire. And why is there only one block of micaceous sandstone?

Having come down firmly in favour of human transport of the bluestones from Mynydd Preselau to Stonehenge, it is necessary to consider three questions which concerned Kellaway and others who have favoured the glacial transport hypothesis:

1. Why did the builders of Stonehenge go all the way to Mynydd Preselau for the bluestones, when there were perfectly satisfactory stones to be had much nearer home?

2. Why, if their main source of bluestones was Mynydd Preselau, did they also bring a single huge block of micaceous sandstone (the Altar Stone), which quite certainly did not come from that area?

3. Why, when they were up on Mynydd Preselau, did they sometimes collect such inferior rocks as the altered volcanic ash which has decayed so badly at Stonehenge, when they could just as easily have brought spotted dolerite every time?

Today, the decision to use bluestones from Mynydd Preselau would have been reached by a committee set up to consider the new building plans for Stonehenge. The committee would have considered the relative merits of sarsen stone and bluestone, and any other stones that might have been proposed, for the type of building planned. They would have considered water transport as compared with overland haulage, and would have worked out possible routes from the different rock sources. But, above all, they would have been working to a budget, and careful costing of the various proposals would probably have been the most important single factor in reaching their final decision.

In Geoffrey's history, Merlin answered the king's question in an entirely different way, which had nothing to do with the building qualities of the stones, nor with the estimated transport costs. Instead he went to some length to describe the seemingly magical healing powers of the stones and their connection with secret religious rites. Geoffrey was eight-and-a-half centuries nearer to the builders of Stonehenge than we are. Is his account correspondingly closer to the actual prehistoric thinking? On questions of this sort, the archaeologist's trowel is generally silent and, if he is to breathe any life into the skeletal records of the past, he must look sideways at the present, rather than backwards in time. The clue may be found hundreds or, more likely, thousands of miles away. The example given below comes from a different culture, in a different continent and a different age. It is not direct evidence, like that of archaeology, but provides a useful guide for argument by analogy.

In the western desert of Australia, there are sacred sites associated with mythical events of the distant past or with ancestral mythical animals, such as the rabbit-eared bandicoot.[4] People who visit these sites collect stones from them, for example, pieces of chert or quartzite, which may be passed on as sacred relics to other members of the tribe and eventually end up hundreds of miles from their source. Here they may be made into arrowheads or tools, even though better quality stone may be available locally. Some pilgrims may be lucky enough to visit the sacred site for themselves. Others have to make do with pieces of the 'true rock' brought back by more fortunate travellers.

The sacred site hypothesis for the bluestones was proposed by Professor Atkinson in his book on Stonehenge. In a memorable passage, he described how Mynydd Preselau might have come to be a sacred mountain, with a special significance for the Beaker people who opened up the trade route to Ireland along the south coast of Wales.

To the traveller humping his pack along the ridgeways of south Pembrokeshire, its cloud-wrapped summit must have seemed no less the home of gods than did Mount Ida to a voyager in the Cretan Plain; and to the trader returning across the sea from Ireland, shielding his eyes from the spray as he peered across the bows of his laden boat, the same summit would be the first welcome sign of land ahead.[5]

An additional reason suggested by Atkinson for the special status of the spotted dolerite among the Stonehenge people was that some of their fine battle axes were made of the very same rock. It must be admitted, though, that this explanation would work just as well the other way round: the battle axes were made of spotted dolerite because it came from the sacred mountain, just as in the example from Western Australia.

There is one bluestone in Salisbury Museum, whose importance far outweighs its relatively humble appearance. This is the stone found by William Cunnington in Boles Barrow. This barrow is a Neolithic long barrow and was almost certainly completed hundreds of years before the first Beaker trader set eyes on the sacred summit of Mynydd Preselau, before the first bluestones of Stonehenge II were set up, and probably even before the first turf was cut on the site that was to become Stonehenge. And yet this stone, like the majority of the Stonehenge bluestones, is a spotted dolerite, and the argument against glacial transport is just as valid here as at Stonehenge. This bluestone was brought all the way from Mynydd Preselau to Salisbury Plain to be incorporated in the body of a long barrow. There can have been no possible economic reason for this. The structure would have been just as satisfactory without it. Mynydd Preselau, and Carn Meini in particular, must have been a sacred site for centuries before the first bluestone was brought to Stonehenge.

Why a mountain in south-west Wales should have been so important to the inhabitants of the Stonehenge area must perhaps remain a mystery, but Boles Barrow may provide a few hints. Most of the long barrows of this area are 'earth mounds', composed of the chalk dug out of their flanking ditches. In contrast to these, Boles Barrow is a cairn built of sarsen stones heaped up into a ridge. In an area where boulders of any sort are scarce, this type of construction seems decidedly eccentric. It is as if the builders had come from the Highland Zone and were determined to build a *proper* cairn, whatever the cost and whatever the local difficulties might be. The bluestone suggests that they came from Pembrokeshire and brought their traditions of a sacred mountain with them, and even made the journey back home for a special stone for their cairn. Beyond that it can only be pure conjecture. Was Mynydd Preselau the local equivalent of Mount Ararat in an ancient tradition of the flood? Was it there that some legendary ancestor had a memorable religious experience or escaped death in a miraculous manner long since forgotten? We shall never know. For us, it must be sufficient to know that it was a sacred mountain and that its memory was preserved across the centuries, far away on Salisbury Plain.

A sacred site on Mynydd Preselau, however, cannot explain the presence at Stonehenge of a large pillar of micaceous sandstone. Whether from the Cosheston Group or the Senni Beds, one thing is quite certain: the Altar Stone was not brought from Mynydd Preselau. This seeming multiplicity of Welsh sources for the foreign stones of Stonehenge has certainly been one of the factors that has kept the glacial transport hypothesis alive. The problem is more apparent than real, however, and results from lumping all the foreign stones together as bluestones, as if they really did belong to one set. The fact is that the distinction between them is not only petrological, but archaeological as well. The Altar Stone, now fallen, seems to have occupied a position along the axis of Stonehenge: the line along which the midsummer sun rose and, in the opposite direction, the midwinter sun set. It was not just one of the foreign bluestones, but an individual stone, brought to Stonehenge to be erected in a particular place, for a special purpose. What that purpose may have been must be reserved for a later chapter.

It is difficult to leave this problem of the source of the bluestones without a nagging worry about the fact that Geoffrey of Monmouth got it so wrong: 'If you want to grace the burial-place of these men with some lasting monument,' replied Merlin, 'send for the Giant's Ring which is on Mount Killaraus in Ireland.'[6]

There have been various attempts to identify Mount Killaraus in Ireland, including Kildare, Killala and Killare.[7] Since the stones quite certainly did not come from Ireland, it is hardly surprising that none of these carries much conviction. Is Mount Killaraus perhaps an early name for Mynydd Preselau? While perfectly possible, this would be difficult to prove. It may be that Geoffrey simply added 'in Ireland' because, as he would have been well aware, so many Irish place-names begin with the root *kil* (*cill*) meaning church. If Mount Killaraus is a name belonging to a genuine prehistoric tradition, the *cill* root can hardly be translated as church. An alternative and much more plausible translation is 'burial ground'. This leads us to consider possible translations for the rest of the word. *Ar* is a Gaelic word which may be translated as 'slaughter', and *arach* is 'field of slaughter' or 'battle field'. Modern Gaelic and Welsh are both derived from a common prehistoric language and it may very well be that Killaraus (*Cill-arach*) is simply another early name for Stonehenge.

By the time Geoffrey was writing, there was an excess of names for Stonehenge, more or less associated with a variety of historical and legendary traditions. It was the Giant's Ring, built long ago by giants, who were believed to have inhabited Britain before the arrival of Brutus and his followers (a belief necessary to explain megalithic and other sites, and a variety of natural phenomena). It was the Temple of Ambrius, perhaps a memory of its distant prehistoric function. It may also have been Killaraus, a name embodying the legend of the massacre at the Cloister of Ambrius. It was Stonehenge to the Saxons, and remains so to this day. Because it was by no means evident that these names all referred to the same place, Geoffrey's story became somewhat complicated. Siting the original Giant's Ring in Ireland may have been pure invention, not fiction for its own sake, but an attempt to make a sensible story out of all the confused traditions that had survived. Without Geoffrey's story, we would have none of them.

CHAPTER 7

GREEK CONTACTS: THE HYPERBOREANS TESTED

Diodorus Siculus, who introduced us to the Hyperboreans and provided independent dating evidence for their spherical temple, also implied that there was a special relationship between them and the Greeks, especially the Delians and the Athenians. If the spherical temple is to be identified with Stonehenge III, then the Hyperboreans must, at least in part, be the people who were buried in the splendid round barrow cemeteries which are such a prominent feature of the surrounding country. These grave groups are remarkable for the size and variety of barrow types (bell barrows, bowl barrows, disc barrows, pond barrows) and also for the richness of their contents (gold, amber, faience, and a variety of artefacts from overseas). From the very outset, one of the most important features of this Wessex Culture was the range of objects in the grave goods indicating contact with Greece:[1]

Gold mounted amber discs: found in three Wiltshire barrows (one in each): one example from Late Minoan 'Tomb of the Double Axes', Knossos, Crete; not known anywhere else.

Gold plated cones (conical buttons) of shale or amber: found in one Dorset and two Wiltshire barrows: 'a constant feature of Mycenaean grave furniture'.

Gold capped stone beads: found in one Wiltshire barrow: one example also from a more distant barrow at Rochford, Essex; 'essentially Mycenaean'; not known elsewhere in western Europe.

Gold *pointille* dagger hafts: one example from Wiltshire (Bush

Gold ornaments from Wessex Culture burials: Bush Barrow (left), Upton
Lovell G2, Wiltshire (centre), and Clandon, Dorset (right)

Barrow); similar dagger hafts from Mycenae and elsewhere in Greece;
also found in Brittany.

Gold cups: one example from a round barrow at Rillaton, Cornwall;
two similar gold cups from Shaft-Grave IV at Mycenae.

Crescentic necklaces of strings of amber beads held apart by multiper-
forate space plates: fragments found in three Wiltshire barrows: also
fragments from three Mycenaean burials: Shaft-Grave IV, Shaft-Grave
Omicron, and Tholos A at Kakovatos.

Segmented faience beads: found in twenty-five Wessex round barrows; possibly of Egyptian origin, also found at Mycenae and Knossos;
virtually unknown in western Europe outside Britain.

Dentated bone mounts: found in one Wiltshire barrow (Bush
Barrow), originally attached to the wooden haft of a mace; very similar bone mounts from Grave Circle B at Mycenae.

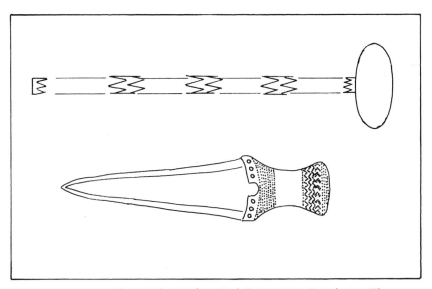

Stone mace and bronze daggers from Bush Barrow, near Stonehenge. The former wooden handles of these objects were ornamented respectively with dentated bone mounts and gold pointille decoration

As Professor Piggott remarked, in his original account of the Wessex Culture, 'such resemblances may be individually fortuitous, but in their cumulative effect are too remarkable to dismiss'. Furthermore, Stonehenge itself is the site of two more Mycenaean correlations. The construction of the trilithons, with the lintels secured in place by mortice and tenon joints, is exactly paralleled in the Postern Gate at Mycenae. The carving of a dagger on Stone 53 is quite unlike any contemporary British type, but shows marked similarity to daggers from the Mycenaean shaft graves.[2]

If the Greek connections were as good as they seem, the Wessex Culture could hardly be bettered as an archaeological record of the Hyperboreans. Unfortunately, the validity of many of these links has been called into question during the last two decades. This has been due, in large part, to improvements in radiocarbon dating, particularly the calibration of the radiocarbon time-scale with the aid of dated tree rings from the extraordinarily long-lived bristle cone pines of California.[3]

When the Wessex Culture was first described by Professor Piggott, more than fifty years ago, our prehistoric ancestors were widely viewed as rather primitive barbarians, living at the very outermost edge of the known world, far removed from the thriving centres of civilization around the eastern Mediterranean. The Mycenaean connection not only provided valuable dating evidence (shaft graves dating from 1600 to 1500 BC), but also gave a convenient explanation for Stonehenge itself, which could hardly have been designed and built by a people who, for all their wealth, were still 'essentially barbarians'.[4]

The idea of a Mycenaean architect for Stonehenge, or at least some Mycenaean influence on its design and construction, did not survive the radiocarbon revolution. We now know that Stonehenge III was built several centuries too early to have benefited from any Mycenaean inspiration. Stonehenge was without question the brainchild of a prehistoric British architect and it stands as a lasting memorial to his genius. While radiocarbon dating was providing a chronological demonstration of British innovation, evidence was also accumulating that the natives of these islands were competent mathematicians, with an impressive grasp of applied geometry,[5] and also very capable observational astronomers, with a particularly detailed knowledge of the motions of the sun and moon.[6] The primitive barbarian image was slowly being replaced by something much more akin to the Hyperboreans who were on such friendly terms with the Delians and the Athenians.

The effect of the calibrated radiocarbon (C–14) chronology on the other links with Mycenae was clearly stated by Professor Colin Renfrew in a paper boldly entitled 'Wessex without Mycenae':

> Since we are now proposing to date the Wessex culture from 2100 BC to 1700 BC, while Late Helladic I, the first phase of the Mycenaean culture, begins about 1600 BC, the whole framework of supposed synchronisms for the Northern European Early Bronze Age, stretching across Europe to Mycenae, collapses. One has the simple choice either of retaining it and rejecting the C–14 calibration *in toto*, or of accepting the C–14 dates, at least tentatively, and following the consequences through.[7]

This looks like a pretty stark choice, with little room for compromise. More than two decades later, it is quite clear that the radiocarbon dates are here to stay and, whatever minor adjustments may be made, the Wessex Culture was drawing to a close (even if not actually finished) before the time of the Mycenaean shaft graves. The particular synchronisms which are under attack, as far as the present discussion is concerned, are between possessions buried with the dead in Wessex and similar objects in Mycenaean graves. But trade, or whatever other contact there may have been between Wessex and Mycenae, was achieved by the living. At either end of every archaeological link between the two areas there lies an uncertain relationship between the property of the living and the goods deposited with the dead. Before reaching any final decisions about the supposed synchronisms, this relationship must be examined.

The richness of the Wessex Culture graves is well known and the gold objects from Bush Barrow, in particular, have been illustrated in many books, most recently alongside a coloured representation of the Bush Barrow 'warrior' himself, standing outside Stonehenge.[8] Very few Wessex burials can compete with this, and only about fifteen per cent of the barrows listed in the original account of the Wessex Culture contained any gold at all. There is also an unexpected element of economy in the grave goods of many Wessex burials. Complete necklaces, for example, are rare. Instead, they are generally represented by a sample of the beads which would have been used in the actual necklace or necklaces (tokenism) – one bead of each material (amber, faience, jet, etc), for example, or perhaps one of each different shape.[9]

The gold objects attributed to the Wessex Culture are rightly admired for their superb craftsmanship. Perhaps rather unexpectedly, although the source of the gold certainly lay outside Wessex (in Ireland, or perhaps North Wales or Scotland), the objects themselves were of local manufacture. Not only that, but there is strong evidence that most of them were the work of a single master craftsman.[10] It has been argued from this that the Wessex Culture as a whole was of relatively short duration. Quite apart from the fact that such a short chronology for the Wessex Culture runs counter to other evidence for its duration, the argument itself is inherently fallacious. If indeed much of the gold-work was the product of a single master craftsman, all that we can properly conclude is that the habit of depositing gold objects as grave goods was very short-lived. In other words, the use of similar objects by the living *may have* long outlasted the practice of burying them with the dead. Is there any evidence to suggest that this is any more than just a possibility?

The round barrows themselves are impressive monuments to the status and power of the people who were buried in them. Like the pyramids of Egypt, each of these round barrows was constructed, at considerable cost to the community, for the burial of a single individual. The cremated remains of lesser individuals might be deposited as secondary burials in the great barrows of their masters, thus acquiring a good position in the afterlife at relatively low cost. There is, however, little correlation between the splendour (size or special design) of the barrows and the richness of their contents.[11] The deposition of rich grave goods, in other words, was not a universal custom among the great men and women of the Wessex Culture. The link between the wealth of the living and the material possessions of the dead is not a simple one.

At the other end of the Wessex–Greek connection lie the Mycenaean shaft graves. In these graves there is a far greater profusion of gold objects than in the British burials and, from the Mycenaean point of view, the Wessex Culture link is quite insignificant. The golden face masks of Mycenae have no parallel in Wessex. The magnificent gold-plated sword handles and the richly ornamented gold diadems from the shaft graves are, artistically, quite unlike the gold-plated dagger pommel and the lozenge-shaped and rectangular plates from Wessex. In Mycenae, the decoration is exuberant and curvilinear, whereas in Wessex, it is economical, precise and linear. The goldsmiths of the two areas were poles apart.

How did the Mycenaean kings become so rich and how can we account for the appearance of Wessex Culture artefacts in their graves, when the historical sources indicate that the link was between the Hyperboreans and the Delians and Athenians? Homer gives more than a hint of the answer in the *Iliad*.[12] Achilles, speaking to Odysseus, says:

I have captured twelve towns from the sea, besides eleven that I took by land in the deep-soiled realm of Troy. From each I got a splendid haul of loot, the whole of which I brought back and gave to my Lord Agamemnon son of Atreus, who had stayed behind in the ships, and who, when I handed it over, gave a little of it out, in bits, but kept the lion's share.

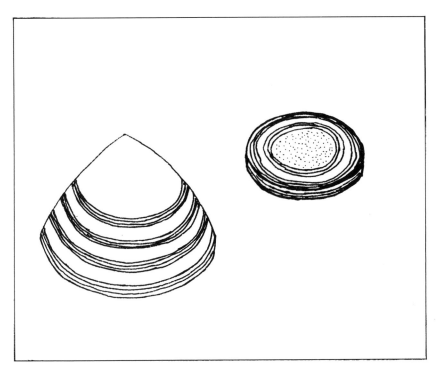

Gold-plated cone and amber disc from Wilsford Barrow G8, Wiltshire
(above) and gold pommel mount from Ridgeway Barrow 7, Dorset (below)

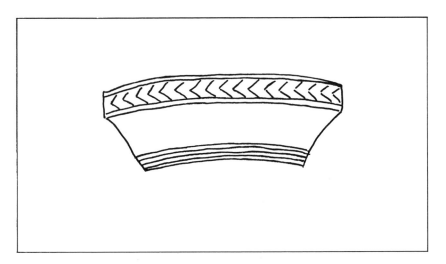

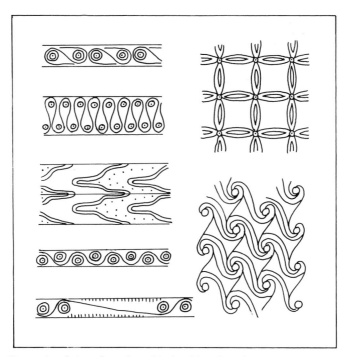

Decorative designs from the gold-plated handles of Mycenaean swords

Agamemnon was King of Mycenae and overlord of the whole of Greece. Earlier in the *Iliad*, a disaffected soldier, Thersites, gives Agamemnon a piece of his mind:

What more do you want? Your huts are full of bronze, and, since we always give you the first pick when a town is sacked, you have plenty of the choicest women in them too. Maybe you are short of gold, the ransom that some Trojan lord may come along with from the city to free a son of his who has been tied up and brought in by myself or another of the men.

Or, as Odysseus says to Achilles, in an attempt to persuade him to return to the attack on Troy:

Later if the gods permit us to sack the great city of Priam, you must come in with us when we are sharing out the spoils, load your ship with gold and bronze to your heart's content, and pick out twenty Trojan women for yourself.

The tiny island of Delos, enriched by gifts to its famous Temple of Apollo, would have been an inviting target for Agamemnon's ancestors and their marauding fleets of Mycenaean pirates. Some of its treasures may have been of considerable antiquity, some perhaps even dating back to its foundation. It is likely too, that the temple treasury would have contained gifts from the Hyperboreans, who were so closely associated with it from the beginning. And, if Agamemnon's behaviour is anything to go by, the Mycenaean kings are unlikely to have had much respect for Apollo or his priests. The *Iliad* begins with a description of an encounter between Agamemnon and a priest of Apollo.

It was Apollo, Son of Zeus and Leto, who started the feud, when he punished the King for his discourtesy to Chryses, his priest, by inflicting a deadly plague on his army and destroying his men. Chryses had come to the Achaean (Greek) ships to recover his captured daughter. He brought with him a generous ransom and carried the chaplet of the Archer-god Apollo on a golden staff in his hand.

Agamemnon was unimpressed by the ransom and sent the priest packing:

'Old man,' he said, 'do not let me catch you loitering by the hollow ships today, nor coming back again, or you may find the god's staff and chaplet a very poor defence. Far from agreeing to set your daughter free, I intend her to grow old in Argos, in my house, a long way from her own country, working at the loom and sharing my bed. Off with you now, and do not provoke me if you want to save your skin.'

The literary evidence does not tell, in so many words, that the Temple of Apollo on Delos was sacked by Mycenaean raiders and its treasures acquired by the king. Nor did the archaeological evidence ever really tells us that Wessex Culture traders were exchanging valuables with the Mycenaeans and that these valuables were immediately buried in the graves of the kings. Combining the archaeological and historical evidence, it is abundantly clear that there is no need to abandon the Greek connection simply because radiocarbon dating has shown that the Wessex Culture is, in large part, earlier than the Mycenaean shaft graves.

One of the most remarkable things suggested by the historical sources is the operation of a prehistoric postal service right across Europe. In the time of Herodotus, it was possible to send parcels from Britain to Greece, with a reasonable expectation of their safe arrival, and this service had probably been in operation for at least a thousand years. Herodotus tells us that the Hyperboreans were in the habit of sending gifts to the Delians, wrapped in straw and passed from hand to hand along a great network of communications, until they reached their destination. He even gives details of the last thousand miles or so of the route by which they were carried. How did he come by these details?

If we wish to send a parcel through the post today, to any destination in the world, all we have to do is wrap it securely, address it correctly and pay the appropriate postage. In the Bronze Age, when the Hyperboreans first started sending their parcels to the Delians, the operators of the postal service were illiterate; they were probably still illiterate in the time of Herodotus. An address written on the outside of the parcel would have been useless. Instead, the name of the sender, the route by which the parcel was to be carried, and the name of the recipient, all had to be memorized by every carrier on the route. All these details, faithfully learnt by heart, arrived with the parcel, so that they could be reversed for the reply; and so the correspondence was maintained. Herodotus not only gives a fascinating insight into the operation of a preliterate postal service, but also provides data which can be checked against the archaeological record.

> Certain sacred offerings wrapped up in wheat straw come from the Hyperboreans into Scythia, whence they are taken over by the neighbouring peoples in succession until they get as far west as the Adriatic: from thence they are sent south, and the first Greeks to receive them are the Dodonaeans. Then, continuing southwards, they reach the Malian gulf, cross to Euboea, and are passed on from town to town as far as Carystus. Then they skip Andros, the Carystians take them to Tenos, and the Tenians to Delos. That is how these things are said to reach Delos at the present time.[13]

Following this route in reverse, a Bronze Age traveller would eventually reach the Danube, long recognized as one of the main prehistoric highways across Europe.[14] Continuing his journey up the Danube, the traveller would enter the territory of an important central European people, somewhere near Vienna. This people, known to archaeology as the Unetice (sometimes Aunjetitz) Culture, occupied an area comprising northern Austria, central and western Czechoslovakia (Moravia, Bohemia), and parts of eastern Germany (Saxony) and south-western Poland (Silesia). This country, centred on the watershed between the Danube (flowing into the Black Sea), the Elbe (flowing into the North Sea), and the Oder (flowing into the Baltic), was at the hub of a great network of European communications; and these communications extended westwards as far as Britain.

Wessex Culture graves have yielded a small number of highly distinctive bronze pins of Unetician types, and also a few remarkable pendants in the form of miniature Unetician halberds, with blades of bronze set in hafts of amber or wood, bound in gold.[15] These connections between the Wessex Culture and the Unetice Culture are well established and have not been affected by improvements in radiocarbon dating. Faience beads, including segmented forms like those found in Wessex, have been found in graves of the Unetice Culture. But the origin of these beads, once seen as 'the exact counterparts of those gaudy glass beads, strung on lengths of copper wire, which were carried as trade goods by the Western explorers of Africa in the nineteenth century',[16] is no longer certain. The most exacting analytical investigations have failed to prove their Egyptian origin, or to disprove the alternative hypothesis that they were manufactured in several centres, including Britain and central Europe.[17]

The link between the Wessex Culture and the central European Unetice Culture provides a connection through to the Danube and thence to that part of the postal route to Delos recorded by Herodotus. This, together with the Greek connection in the Mycenaean shaft graves and elsewhere, shows that the historical sources are not misleading us.

The links of the Wessex Culture with central Europe and, beyond that, with Greece, are of the greatest importance archaeologically and also, in connection with the Hyperboreans, historically. But geographically and culturally, the closest overseas link was with Brittany. Is it

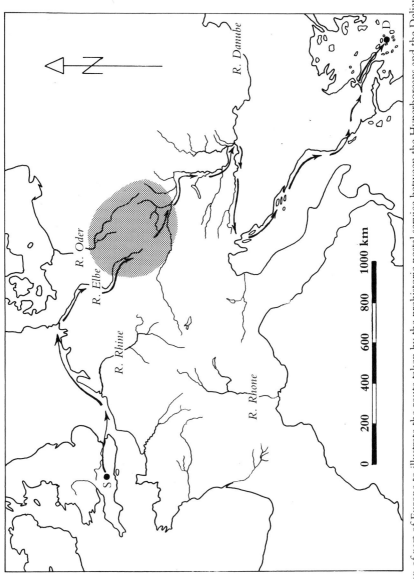

Map of part of Europe to illustrate the route taken by the prehistoric postal service between the Hyperboreans and the Delians

coincidence that Brittany (Armorica) occupies such an important place in Geoffrey of Monmouth's history? King Arthur's great uncle, Aldroenus, and his own chief ally, Hoel, were both kings of the Armorican Britons. Unfortunately there is no possibility of testing this connection, because it was also genuinely important in the post-Roman period, to which the Arthurian stories had become attached long before Geoffrey wrote his history.

CHAPTER 8

PREHISTORIC CLIMATE: DIODORUS TESTED

The weather is a subject of almost universal interest, and never more so than when you are travelling abroad. Before you leave, there is the problem of deciding what clothes to take, and then, when you get back home, everyone wants to know what the weather was like. The Greeks, who visited the island of the Hyperboreans, brought back an account of the weather which has been preserved for us by Diodorus. They said that the climate was so temperate that the Hyperboreans could gather two harvests in a year. In another book, Diodorus also describes the climate of Britain as being extremely cold. If the island of the Hyperboreans really was Britain, these contrasting descriptions of the climate require some explanation.

A simple explanation, suggested by the historical and archaeological evidence discussed in the last few chapters, would be that the two descriptions were not contemporary. The very temperate climate belongs to a period between 2000 and 1500 BC, whereas the extremely cold climate was much later, probably about 300 BC. Historical evidence for climatic changes during the last thousand years indicates that such an explanation would be perfectly plausible. We know, for example, that there was a warm period, between about AD 1000 and 1250, which enabled the Vikings to colonize Greenland. We also know that, a few centuries later, there was an extremely cold period, between 1550 and 1700, which caused a 'Little Ice Age', with considerable advances of glaciers in many mountain areas.[1] If a comparable climatic change could be demonstrated for prehistoric Britain between about 1500 BC and 300 BC, the historical sources for the British Bronze Age would have passed yet another test.

The history of the British climate since the last glaciation is written in the peat bogs. These damp, largely organic, deposits are renowned for the wonderful preservation of organic remains, even including occasional dramatic discoveries of human bodies, complete with skin, hair and clothing (bog people),[2] of whom the Danish Tollund man and, more recently, the English Lindow man are perhaps the best-known examples. The peat bogs, though they do not themselves support much in the way of tree growth, do provide a repository for the vast quantities of pollen grains which are carried on the wind from adjacent forested areas. Analysis of the pollen successions from many peat bogs has revealed the changing composition of the forests, which covered much of the country in prehistoric times. Birch woods were the first to colonize the cold wasteland left behind by the retreating ice. As the climate improved, these were overtaken by pine; and the pine, in turn, gave way to deciduous forests, generally dominated by oak, but also containing alder, elm and lime.

The deciduous forests were established well before 5000 BC, more than two thousand years before the first turf was cut on the site that was to become Stonehenge. Thereafter, the changes in forest composition become more subtle and less easy to interpret in terms of climatic variation. Human activity, particularly agriculture and forest clearance, was beginning to make its mark on the environment and was undoubtedly registered in the tree pollen succession.[3] Fortunately, there is more to the stratigraphy of peat bogs than pollen grains.

Forty miles or so west of Stonehenge, the peat bogs of the Somerset Levels, near Glastonbury, have yielded a wealth of archaeological material, ranging in age from Neolithic to Roman. Of particular interest in the present context are the wooden trackways which have been found at the boundary between two quite distinct types of peat. The trackways, made of timbers and brushwood, were fixed in place by vertical piles driven into the underlying peat. Many of the timbers retained distinctive marks of the Late Bronze Age socketed axes with which they had been felled, and radiocarbon dating shows that the tracks were laid between 1100 and 600 BC.[4]

The dark compact peat below the tracks is a well humified *Sphagnum* peat, with abundant heather (*Calluna*) and patches of bog cotton (*Eriophorum*), but hardly any sedges (*Carex*). From this familiar flora, we can deduce a poor acid soil, whose only source of water was the

mineral-deficient rainfall from above. Conditions on the ground would
have been quite dry enough for walking. Above the tracks, the paler less
compact peat is dominated by the giant sword sedge (*Cladium mariscus*),
which grows to a height of six feet and forms dense beds in the fens of
East Anglia at the present time. *Sphagnum, Calluna* and *Eriophorum* are
all absent from this upper peat layer. The change could hardly have been
more complete: a dry acid soil had given way to a lime-rich fen. The
reason is not in any doubt. Greatly increased rainfall resulted in extensive flooding of the bog surface with lime-rich river water from the
adjacent hills.[5]

The tracks themselves were an attempt by the local inhabitants to
maintain their familiar pathways across the heath, by building them up
above the encroaching water level. Like so many other attempts to combat the forces of nature, it was doomed to failure. The tracks were soon
submerged, buried beneath the accumulating fen peat, and preserved for
posterity. The people, however, were not defeated by this setback. Ever
resourceful, they became amphibious, and having established the famous
lake villages of Glastonbury and Meare, proceeded to travel across their
former heath in dug-out canoes! Such a dug-out was found in the
Cladium peat at Shapwick and has been radiocarbon dated to about 450
BC.[6] It is quite clear that the wooden trackways were constructed during
a period of transition from a relatively dry climate to a much wetter one.
But how can we compare this with the climates recorded by Diodorus,
when he says nothing whatever about rainfall, and the peat bogs give no
obvious indication of change in temperature at this level?

Having established the reality of the climatic change between about
1100 and 600 BC, it is necessary to return to the tree pollen record for
further details. The changes that were taking place during this period
include a decrease in the proportion of oak, lime and alder, and a corresponding marked increase in birch, together with the arrival of a significant amount of beech. Birch is a fast growing tree and is quick to colonize open land which has gone to waste. Its increase can thus be
explained by continuing forest clearance, combined with relatively inefficient agriculture. Beech, on the other hand, is a slow grower, and its
establishment as a significant component of the British forests can hardly
be attributed to human intervention. In southern Scandinavia, the
spread of beech was accompanied by a similar increase in spruce. This

was long ago interpreted as the result of a change from dry, warm, continental conditions to a cooler and wetter climate.[7]

The correlation between recent climatic change in Britain and the advance and retreat of glaciers elsewhere has already been mentioned. In view of this, the recent find of an early Bronze Age man in an alpine glacier is of the greatest interest. In the current phase of global warming, widely attributed to the greenhouse effect, the glaciers in the Alps and elsewhere are retreating. The body, partly exposed by the melting ice, was discovered in September 1991, at a height of about 3,200 m on the Similaun Glacier, about 60 km south-south-west of Innsbruck. It had been preserved in deep-freeze conditions ever since the man died, probably about 2000 BC. According to the newspaper report:

> He was wearing leather leggings and footwear made of bark and leather stuffed with straw and fur to protect him from the extreme cold. He was clutching a metal-headed axe and was equipped with a leather quiver carrying 12 stone- and bronze-tipped arrows, a knife with a stone blade and a pouch of flints.[8]

After he died, the climate must have deteriorated until his body was encased in such a thick layer of ice that no subsequent warming has ever been able to reach it until now.

The climatic change we have been considering brought to a close a period of several thousand years, long known in north-western Europe as the Climatic Optimum. Pollen data from sites right across Europe have been used to produce a map of the mean July temperatures during this period).[9] The samples used in this analysis are dated to about 4000 BC, a time when the natural forests were as yet unaffected by the inroads of human activity. The mean July temperature in Britain was about 2°C higher than today.

The visitors to prehistoric Britain, whose climatic observations are recorded by Diodorus, knew nothing about mean July temperatures and, in any case, had no means of measuring the temperature. The climatic information they brought home was an impression of what the weather felt like, compared to the weather at home. At the present time, the mean July temperature in Greece is about 10°C higher than in Britain.[10] During the Climatic Optimum, while the mean July temperature in

Britain was 2°C higher than today, that in Greece was about 2°C lower.[11] The temperature difference (in summer) between Greece and Britain was thus only about 6°C during the Climatic Optimum, and the British climate might well have been described as temperate by a Greek visitor. Later visitors would have noticed a far greater difference in temperature, the reverse of what so many British holiday-makers experience along the northern shores of the Mediterranean today, and they would have had good reason to describe the British climate as extremely cold.

The evidence of prehistoric climates, like that of archaeology and astronomy, supports the view that Diodorus, in recording what he himself referred to as 'ancient myths', has preserved for us a genuine tradition of exchange visits between the Greeks and the Britons as long ago as the Bronze Age. These visits took place at a time when the Wessex Culture was at its height and Stonehenge was the greatest temple in the land.

PART III
THE GREAT AGE OF STONEHENGE

CHAPTER 9

MERLIN:
ARCHITECT OF STONEHENGE

The quest for King Arthur in the fifth and sixth centuries AD, while it has to some extent lightened the darkness of those dark ages of British history, has signally failed to establish Arthur's own place there. The only alternative to abandoning the search altogether was to make a careful study of a few scraps of evidence, generally disregarded by scholars as being either pure fiction or unhistorical myth. These are the connections between the Arthurian dynasty and Stonehenge recorded by Geoffrey of Monmouth. Combining these with the account of the Hyperboreans and their spherical temple, given by Diodorus Siculus, a picture emerges of a period of British prehistory, which might well be referred to as 'the Great Age of Stonehenge', when the fame of this great temple was sufficient to attract visitors from as far afield as Greece. Not only is this picture internally consistent, but it stands up to a variety of archaeological and scientific tests. This was an age great enough to be the ultimate source for the legends of King Arthur.

Geoffrey's account of the Arthurian dynasty begins immediately after the departure of the Romans. The three most important characters in the early part of this story are the evil, scheming usurper, Vortigern; the noble and rightful king, Aurelius Ambrosius; and the mysterious prophet and builder of Stonehenge, Merlin. Each of these characters, by the time he finally arrived on the pages of Geoffrey's history and became to that extent fixed, was probably compound.

Vortigern is, in part, a genuine fifth-century ruler, whose deeds and misdeeds are recorded by Gildas and Nennius, and, in part, a prehistoric (legendary) figure, who was involved in the disaster at the Temple of Ambrius, which took place about 1500 BC. Aurelius Ambrosius, who is more usually just called Aurelius and, once, Ambrosius, is clearly identified by Geoffrey with the fifth-century British hero, referred to as Ambrosius Aurelianus by Gildas, and Ambrosius by Nennius. He is, however, also the prehistoric king responsible for building Stonehenge (Stonehenge III), about 2000 BC. We have already seen that Geoffrey's King Arthur may himself have originated as a legendary (prehistoric) hero, to whose name the exploits of Magnus Maximus, in the fourth century AD, and Aurelius Ambrosianus, in the fifth century AD, had become attached.

Merlin too is a compound character, though, unlike the other two, neither component is connected with the real history of the fifth century AD. He first appears as a boy prophet, discovered by Vortigern after the disaster at the Temple of Ambrius, about 1500 BC; then, in a later chapter, he reappears as the architect and engineer in charge of building Stonehenge, which is of course the very same Temple of Ambrius, about 2000 BC. The chronological reversal is not as serious as it seems. Geoffrey collected individual stories and traditions, and blended them into a continuous narrative. Where he and Nennius collected the same stories, as for example that of the boy prophet, they are not always presented in the same place in the sequence of events.

Stonehenge III is unique. It is and has been for thousands of years one of the wonders of Britain. At the time of its construction, however, its unique character may have been somewhat less striking than it is today. Then, it was simply the only example in stone of a type of building which may have been quite familiar in timber. It has been remarked many times that the mortice and tenon joints, by which the lintels are fixed to their uprights, and the tongue and groove joints, by which they are keyed to one another, are familiar structural features in woodwork. It is too early, by several centuries, to have been based on a Mycenean model, such as the Postern Gate, whose lintel is known to be attached to its uprights by mortice and tenon joints. Stonehenge III was therefore quite independently modelled on a timber prototype.

In Geoffrey of Monmouth's account of the building of Stonehenge, Aurelius wanted 'a novel building which would stand for ever'. When his carpenters and stonemasons, from all parts of the country, had failed to come up with a suitable design, Merlin was summoned and produced the plans for Stonehenge III. Merlin's design was a masterpiece. The limited life-span of timber buildings was already well known from such structures as Woodhenge. The obvious answer to this problem was to substitute stone for wood. Merlin's genius was not so much that he thought of this, but that he persuaded the king that he could put it into effect.

All the engineering skills and craftsmanship required for building Stonehenge had been in use for centuries. Large stones had been dragged across the country to the sites of hundreds of earlier stone circles. Standing stones had been set up in holes deep enough to ensure their permanent stability. Massive cap stones had been lifted up to cover the passages and chambers of megalithic tombs. Stone had been shaped to the most exacting standards in the manufacture of axes, maceheads, battle axes and axe hammers. Building Stonehenge demanded no new technology: just a scaling up of existing skills. If large stones could be hauled for short distances, larger ones could be hauled for greater distances. It would just require more men and more time. If small stones could be sculpted to almost any desired shape, so too could much larger ones. What the construction of Stonehenge required, above all else, was outstanding administrative ability and almost unlimited resources of manpower. Merlin had the ability and the king had the resources. It was a powerful combination.

'Now hang on', you might be saying. 'Just a moment. You are talking about Merlin as if he was a real person. Are you serious?' That is a good question, and a familiar one too. Did Shakespeare write the complete works of William Shakespeare, or was it Francis Bacon who wrote them? Was Geoffrey of Monmouth the real author of the *Historia Regum Britanniae*? Was the *Historia Brittonum* really compiled by Nennius? Did St Paul really write all the epistles attributed to him? Was there ever really an early Greek poet called Homer, who wrote the *Iliad* and the *Odyssey*? Such questions are an integral part of the academic games some people play. Let play begin!

In a sense these questions are irrelevant. Hamlet, the Epistles of St Paul, the *Iliad*, and Stonehenge all exist and can be appreciated, whether or not we know who was responsible for them. What's in a name anyway? Someone masterminded the construction of Stonehenge, of that there can be no doubt. Is calling him Merlin doing anything more than simply giving that very real person a label? If the answer to this question is yes, read on; we still have a long way to go. If the answer is no, then the Roman conquest of Britain, for example, would be reduced to the arrival of samian ware and central heating on the archaeological scene: no Julius Caesar, no Claudius; no Aulus Plautius, Vespasian or Agricola; no Cassivellaunus, Caratacus or Boudicca; no Brigantes or Iceni; just buildings and pottery; floors and occupation layers; construction, destruction and decay. What would we have called them? The Hypocaust People?

Names and the people they belong to are an essential part of the distinction between history and prehistory. Calling the builder of Stonehenge Merlin carries with it the implication that there is a faint glimmer of history reaching up to us from those dark and distant depths of our prehistoric past. Can this be true? In answer to this question, it will be instructive to consider the earliest stone architecture of Egypt, which was initiated by King Zoser early in the 3rd Dynasty, about 2650 BC.[1]

King Zoser's famous Step Pyramid at Saqqara was the first of the great series of pyramids, which were built mainly during the next 500 years. Associated with the Step Pyramid are some twenty other stone buildings, the whole complex being surrounded by a 10 m-high stone wall. Most of these buildings were non-functional and were in fact dummies – solid masses of masonry, with representations of doorways carved on the outside. Access to the whole area was gained by one small doorway through the outer wall, but there were fourteen imitation double doorways, each situated in a large solid tower and with corresponding double doorways carved on the inside of the wall. Many of the internal buildings had beautifully carved columns attached to their walls, with capitals in the form of lotus flowers, papyrus flowers or palm leaves. In the few buildings which had genuine interiors, there were passages with stone ceilings carved to resemble log rafters. Stylistic features of these buildings are directly related to the contemporary mud-brick and timber buildings on which they were modelled. Sometimes too, as at Stonehenge, there is structural evidence of a timber prototype.

Stonehenge and King Zoser's Saqqara complex of stone buildings are parallel, but otherwise quite unrelated, examples of early stone architecture based on the less durable models current at the time. Both were built in an attempt to ensure permanence. These two early examples of architecture in stone were applied to projects considered by their builders to be far more important than the mere habitation or security of mortal men: at Stonehenge, a temple to the immortal gods and, at Saqqara, a palace and all the other accommodation required for the immortal soul of a departing king. They were also monuments to the status and achievements of the kings, visible for all the world to see and durable enough to carry the message far across the centuries into the future.

The architect of the Step Pyramid and the whole Saqqara complex, in which it is set, was Imhotep. The importance of Imhotep in Egyptian history and tradition may be gathered from Manetho's account of the 3rd Dynasty in his *History of Egypt*, written in Greek about 270 BC:[2]

The Third Dynasty comprised nine kings of Memphis.

1. Necherophes, for 28 years. In his reign the Lybians revolted against Egypt, and when the moon waxed beyond reckoning, they surrendered in terror.

2. Tosorthros [Zoser], for 29 years. In his reign lived Imuthes [Imhotep], who because of his medical skill had the reputation of Asclepios [the Greek god of medicine] among the Egyptians, and who was the inventor of the art of building with hewn stone. He also devoted attention to writing.

Of the remaining seven kings of this dynasty, Manetho merely recorded their names and the lengths of their reigns. Just as Merlin, the builder of Stonehenge, is a major character in Geoffrey of Monmouth's history; so Imhotep, the builder of Saqqara, receives more attention in Manetho's history than any of the kings of the Third Dynasty. Clearly the creation of great and lasting architecture in stone for the first time was something which caught the popular imagination and thereby found its way into the national memory. Manetho was writing about 2,400 years after the building of the Step Pyramid, but as an Egyptian high priest, he will not only have had access to extensive temple libraries, but also the ability to interpret their records.

King lists, such as the 'Papyrus of the Kings' now in Turin Museum, will have been prominent among the early sources used by Manetho. This papyrus, dating from the reign of Rameses II, about 1250 BC, refers to Imhotep as the 'master builder who causes people to live'. It also contains the first mention of him as son of the god Ptah by a mortal woman called Kherdw'ankh. The Papyrus of the Kings, while a thousand years earlier than Manetho, is still some 2,400 years later than the building of the Saqqara complex. Much more important than these texts in ensuring Imhotep's continuing reputation as one of the world's all time great architects, are hieroglyphic texts carved in stone and uncovered during archaeological excavations. At Saqqara itself, the base of a royal statue bears an incomplete hieroglyphic text including the words 'Imhotep, carpenter, sculptor'! The long standing Egyptian tradition that Imhotep was the originator of architecture in stone is appropriately confirmed by a contemporary text carved on stone.

By the time Imhotep acquired the status of a demigod, as the son of Ptah, his reputation extended well beyond the field of architecture. He was believed to have been the founder of a school of philosophy, to have been a writer of distinction, and to have had considerable skills in the field of medicine. By the sixth century BC, he had become a true god. Temples were built in his honour and bronze images, showing him seated with a roll of papyrus in one hand, were widely distributed. He was considered to be a patron of the scribes, and his temples were visited particularly by the sick and by barren women.

How Imhotep, the architect of Saqqara, acquired his posthumous reputation as a philosopher, writer and physician is by no means clear. It is possible that he was indeed all these things in his own lifetime. There may, on the other hand, have been other Imhoteps, perhaps named after him, whose careers gradually merged with his, as their individual traditions receded into the mists of time. There may also have been an element of invention involved, the story growing as it was told and retold across the centuries. Whatever the explanation, the role of the later Imhotep as patron of the scribes and healer of the sick far outshone the memory of the original Imhotep as the builder of Saqqara.

Imhotep and Merlin have much in common, but there is one glaring difference between them. Imhotep's reputation as a great architect is almost universally recognized and there are full accounts of him in all the standard works of reference. On Merlin's great achievement at Stonehenge, however, these same books remain silent. Of course the reason is not far to seek. The name of Imhotep appears in early hieroglyphic inscriptions, including that on the contemporary royal statue at Saqqara. Without these hieroglyphic records, the later texts would have had little impact. Who would have taken the demigod Imhotep, son of Ptah, seriously, as the builder of the Saqqara complex, when the earliest reference to him was 1,400 years later than the building in question? No one. Without the early hieroglyphic records, the legend of Imhotep would have no more impact on the history of architecture than that of Merlin.

Geoffrey's Merlin has a number of characteristics in common with the Imhotep of later Egyptian tradition. He had no earthly father, but his mother was a nun and a daughter of the King of Demetia. He was renowned for his prophecies, made at the request of King Vortigern. He was well versed in healing, knowing the value of different herbal remedies, as well as the healing properties of certain megalithic stones. He was a skilled engineer, dismantling and re-erecting the Giant's Ring with the aid of 'all the gear he considered necessary'. Finally, he was a magician, able with the aid of secret drugs to alter the appearance of a man so completely that he would pass for anyone else he wished. His services were highly valued by three successive kings, Vortigern, Aurelius and Utherpendragon. Like the later Imhotep, his architectural and engineering skills are accorded scant attention in comparison with his prophecies.

Merlin first appears in Geoffrey's history at the end of Vortigern's reign, after the massacre at the Cloister of Ambrius. Vortigern had fled to the hills and was endeavouring to build himself a strong defensive tower, but each night the foundations which had been laid during the day were swallowed up in the ground and disappeared. Vortigern was beginning to panic and summoned his magicians to ask their advice. They recommended that he should find a boy without a father, kill him, and sprinkle his blood on the mortar and stones. Only in this way would the foundations hold firm. So messengers were sent throughout the land to find such a boy. Eventually they came to a place where there were some boys playing by the town gate. While they watched, two of the boys began to argue and one taunted the other with the words 'As for you, nobody knows who you are, for you never had a father!'[3] The messengers lost no time in questioning Merlin, for such was the boy's name, and his mother, who was daughter of a king of Demetia and lived in St Peter's church in the same town, with some nuns. The messengers returned to the king, taking Merlin and his mother with them. The mother's story, as related to the king, is worth quoting:

When I was in our private apartments with my sister nuns, some one used to come to me in the form of a most handsome young man. He would often hold me tightly in his arms and kiss me. When he had been some little time with me he would disappear, so that I could no longer see him. Many times, too, when I was sitting alone, he would talk with me, without becoming visible; and when he came to see me in this way he would often make love with me, as a man would do, and in this way he made me pregnant.[4]

Merlin then went up to the king and asked why he and his mother had been summoned before him. So the king explained to him about the foundations of his tower and how his magicians had advised sprinkling them with the blood of a fatherless boy. 'Tell your magicians to appear in front of me', answered Merlin, 'and I will prove that they have lied.'

The king immediately summoned his magicians and allowed Merlin to cross-examine them. In no time at all, he had demonstrated, to the intense embarrassment of the magicians, that the foundations were being weakened by a subterranean pool of water. Then he asked them what lay beneath the pool. When they did not reply, he ordered the pool to be drained and said that they would find two hollow stones at the bottom of it, and inside the stones there would be two dragons, lying asleep. When the pool was drained, the dragons emerged, one white and one red, and began to fight. When the king asked Merlin to interpret the meaning of this battle of the dragons, 'he went into a prophetic trance and spoke'.[5] There follows a long and rambling account of the prophecies of Merlin.

Geoffrey of Monmouth did not invent this remarkable story, nor did he copy it from Nennius, though essentially the same story is included in the *Historia Brittonum*. Geoffrey's fatherless boy is called Merlin throughout the story, except during his meeting with Vortigern's magicians, when he is suddenly referred to as 'Merlin, who was also called Ambrosius' and again as 'Ambrosius Merlin'. In the *Historia Brittonum* he is not named at all, and the king is only named once; but, when he had interpreted the fight between the dragons, the king asked his name and he replied 'I am called Ambrosius'. Nennius then, by way of explanation, adds:

That is, he was shown to be Emrys the Overlord. The king asked 'What family do you come from?' and he answered 'My father is one of the consuls of the Roman people.' So the king gave him the fortress, with all the kingdoms of the western part of Britain.[6]

This explanation makes nonsense of the whole story, which depends on the fact that the boy had no father. Because the boy said that he was called Ambrosius, Nennius, or whoever else added the explanation, presumed that he had to be the Ambrosius who fought with such success against the Saxons, and then, to fit this identification, had the king provide him with a suitable inheritance. Geoffrey was not fooled by this explanation but, in deference to the authority of Nennius, mentioned the fact that Merlin was sometimes called Ambrosius.

Why this confusion about names? Why did the fatherless boy tell the king that he was called Ambrosius, if his name was really Merlin? It is perhaps significant that the confusion arises while Merlin is interpreting the battle of the dragons, while he is, as Geoffrey tells us, in a prophetic trance. A later passage, describing Merlin's introduction to Aurelius, may shed further light on this problem. As soon as Merlin was presented to him, Aurelius 'ordered him to prophesy the future, for he wanted to hear some marvels from him':

'Mysteries of this sort cannot be revealed,' answered Merlin, 'except where there is the most urgent need for them. If I were to utter them as an entertainment, or where there was no need at all, then the spirit which controls me would forsake me in the moment of need.'[7]

It is possible that Merlin the prophet operated as a trance medium. If this were so, and someone asked him his name while he was prophesying, he would give the name of the spirit that was speaking through him, rather than his own name. The difficulty encountered by Geoffrey, when he found that the Merlin of his fatherless boy story was called Ambrosius by Nennius, thus disappears. After the boy's statement that he is called Ambrosius, Nennius adds 'that is he was seen to be Emrys the Overlord (*Embreis Guletic*).' What if 'Emrys the Overlord' was not 'Ambrosius, who was the great king among all the kings of the British nation'[8] in the fifth century, but Ambrius, of the Cloister of Ambrius, whose temple was Stonehenge.

The story of the fatherless boy prophet, as it stands, is not history, and certainly not part of the history of Britain in the fifth century AD. None the less, though not in itself history, the story does have a history of its own, which we may attempt to unravel. It probably originated in the life of a real prophet, whose fame was such that his memory passed into popular tradition. Stories, once they enter folk memory, may develop and grow, or they may gradually be forgotten, as newer or more interesting material is accumulated; they seldom remain static. This story was one of the survivors. Like Imhotep, Merlin's achievements were so great that he had to be supplied with a remarkable start in life. The 'virgin birth' of Merlin (the fatherless boy) is not unlike the origin of the later Imhotep, as the son of a mortal woman by the god Ptah. It raised him above the general level of ordinary mortal humanity.

The dispute between the boy Merlin and the king's magicians brings to mind the visit of the boy Jesus to the temple in Jerusalem.[9] It may have been added at a time when the spread of Christianity seemed to threaten the old ways and memories; as much as to say, 'If your prophet was so clever when he was only a young boy, so was ours!' On the other hand the threat to his life, as a sacrifice to ensure the stability of the king's tower, seems to come from an earlier period. Hiel the Bethelite, about 850 BC, laid the foundations of Jericho in his firstborn son, Abiram, and set up its gates in his youngest son, Segub.[10] Perhaps a century or two later, a man was buried deep in the foundations of an Iron Age rampart at Maiden Castle, the great Dorset hill-fort, at a crucial point in its defences. Sir Mortimer Wheeler, in his excavation report, suggested that this might have been a foundation sacrifice, like those at Jericho.[11]

Merlin the prophet, the real Merlin without all the trimmings, belongs to prehistory. He is neither medieval fiction, nor fifth-century wonder-boy, though elements of both have been added to what was left of his memory. But his story is entirely separate from that of Merlin the builder of Stonehenge, and the two may not have been blended into one until Geoffrey of Monmouth assembled the material for his history. Nennius tells the story of the prophet as an isolated unit, and places it between Part 2 of the Life of Saint Germanus and Part 3 of the *Kentish Chronicle*; but he makes no mention of Merlin the architect at all.

If Geoffrey did not invent the story of Merlin the fatherless boy prophet, it is in the highest degree unlikely that he should have invented the story of Merlin the builder of Stonehenge. He tends to embroider the 'facts' of his history, rather than invent them. He is, for example, deeply imbued with the importance of the nobility: little wonder in a society in which genealogy was the basis of wealth and position. Thus making Merlin's mother the daughter of a king of Demetia is a typical example of Geoffrey's embroidery of the facts; and Vortigern, in spite of the fact that he intends to kill her son, 'received the mother with due courtesy, for he knew she came of a noble family'. For Nennius, the mother had no special identity or ancestry, and once she had made her brief statement to the effect that the boy had no human father, she was dispensed with, and the messengers took the fatherless boy to face the king by himself.

With the Stonehenge story, Geoffrey may well have invented the former existence of the Giant's Ring on Mount Killaraus in Ireland if, as suggested in an earlier chapter, Killaraus (*cill-arach*, the burial ground at the field of slaughter) is simply another name for Stonehenge. If this is so, he must also have invented the expedition of Utherpendragon to fetch the stones from Ireland. But the actual 'fact' that Stonehenge was built by Merlin is not an embroidery of anything. It is so totally unnecessary to the main purpose of Geoffrey's history of the Kings, that it is almost certainly a genuine tradition, and like the Egyptian tradition of Imhotep as the architect of Saqqara, it is overshadowed by the much more popular tradition of 'the other Merlin', the prophet. The building of Stonehenge, like its Egyptian counterpart, must have impressed itself on the people, not only through the genius of the architect, but because of the unparalleled involvement of the whole people in such a vast public engineering project. Unlike Imhotep, there is not the remotest chance of earlier documentary evidence or of contemporary hieroglyphics at Stonehenge. But while Imhotep's reputation is rightly assured by the existence of such texts, should Merlin's be destroyed for the lack of them?

CHAPTER 10

STONEHENGE: BUILDING COSTS

Stonehenge, the Temple of Ambrius, is a monument to the architectural and engineering genius of one man, Merlin. It is also a memorial to the multitudes of people, unlearned and unnamed, who strove and sweated, blistered their hands, battered their knuckles and strained their backs, all in the service of their king and his great project of building a temple which would stand for ever. How many people laboured? For how long? What was the cost of Stonehenge to the society which gave it birth? Did the work have such an effect on the generation that built it, that it entered into folk memory, never to be forgotten?

Fortunately for this enquiry, the builders of Stonehenge and other megalithic monuments in Britain were not the only people who engaged in such activities. Three methods are available for the study of megalithic engineering: (i) examination of the records of early engineering (e.g. Egyptian); (ii) folk memory of more recent megalithic engineering (e.g. Madagascar); (iii) experiments with different methods. The last two methods were wonderfully combined during Thor Heyerdahl's 1955-6 expedition to Easter Island.

Moving the stones

The Egyptians were great illustrators and adorned the walls of tombs and temples with pictures showing all manner of contemporary activities, as well as religious scenes. The tomb of Jehutihetep, a nobleman of the XIIth Dynasty (a little after 2000 BC), contains an illustration showing his own colossal seated statue being pulled along on a sledge. Teams of men are pulling on four ropes attached to the front of the sledge and the statue is securely tied to the sledge with ropes. The foreman is standing on the knees of the moving statue, directing operations, while another man stands on the front of the sledge and pours water down to lubricate its passage. There are men walking alongside carrying further supplies of water and others walking behind, presumably in readiness to relieve the rope teams. The alabaster statue (if the illustration is to scale) probably weighed about 16 tonnes[1] and the sledge is being hauled by 172 men.

Professor Atkinson conducted several experiments on the transport of stones, both overland and by water.[2] For these experiments he used a concrete model of a stone, weighing about 1.5 tonnes. For overland transport, this stone was firmly lashed to a sledge. A gang of thirty-two senior schoolboys could just haul it up a slope of about four degrees (1 in 15). Using rollers underneath the sledge allowed a reduction in the total workforce from thirty-two to twenty-four: fourteen pulling on the rope, eight on ropes attached to the corners of the sledge to prevent it slipping off the rollers; and four moving the rollers from the back to the front of the sledge as it rode over them. For river transport, Atkinson used three canoes made of elm boarding, joined together by four transverse timbers to support the stone, which was then easily punted up and down the River Avon near Salisbury by four schoolboys. This is a telling illustration of the importance of water transport, which continued into recent times. The great network of canals constructed in the eighteenth century only became redundant with the development of rail transport in the nineteenth.

In 1979 J.P. Mohen carried out a number of experiments with a concrete model of the 32-tonne capstone of a chambered tomb at Bougon in France.[3] The block was moved on oak rollers over rails of squared oak trunks. It took 170 people pulling on ropes and thirty more working with levers to move it.

On Easter Island, at the time of Heyerdahl's visit, some of the natives claimed descent from the last of the 'long-ears', who had been the ruling class before the 'statue-overthrowing-time'. Chief among these was Don Pedro Atan, the Mayor of Easter Island, a remarkable character who could recite his pedigree (not always correctly) for eleven generations back to Ororoina, the only long-ear to survive the battle at Iko's ditch. The story of this war involved a great conflagration in the ditch, in which almost all the long-ears were burned to death. This ditch, so well preserved in folk memory, was also visible on the ground. Archaeological excavation, initiated by Heyerdahl, soon revealed a prominent layer of burnt wood some way below the surface, with the adjacent soil baked red by the intense heat of the fire.[4] Radiocarbon dating placed this fire in the middle of the seventeenth century AD, a date in complete accord with Pedro Atan's eleven generations from Ororoina. What else did the mayor 'remember'?

Heyerdahl had asked many of the natives how the giant statues were moved, for distances of anything up to 13 km (8 miles), from the quarries where they were produced. The answer was always the same: they went by themselves. One old woman elaborated on this story by telling of an old witch who lived at Rano Raraku, where the statues were carved out of the rock. By her magic, she breathed life into the statues and made them go wherever they should. Finally, Don Pedro Atan succumbed to Heyerdahl's persistent enquiries:

> 'I believe that they walked', he said, 'and we must respect our fore-fathers who have said that they walked. But the forefathers who told me had not seen it with their own eyes, so who knows if they did not use a *miro manga erua?*'

It then transpired that a *miro manga erua* was a sledge made from a forked tree trunk and that such sledges had certainly been used to transport great blocks for building walls. This was real progress. A feast was arranged. Don Pedro Atan made the arrangements and soon a motley team of 180 natives (men and women) were pulling away at a long rope which had been tied round the neck of a newly excavated statue. Once started, the 12-tonne statue 'slid away over the plain so quickly that Lazarus, the mayor's assistant, jumped up on to the giant's face and stood waving his arms and cheering'.

In Madagascar, a megalithic culture was still flourishing in the nineteenth century and information from living memory was collected by R.P. Callet and others. The largest standing stone in Madagascar is about 8 m (26 ft) long by 1 m (3 ft) wide and must weigh about 10 tonnes. It was pulled on a log sledge and up to 300 people were involved in its transport.[6] When stones were needed for the construction of a new chambered tomb, everyone turned out to pull them: men,

A newly excavated Easter Island statue being hauled across
country

women and children. One man would ride on top of the stone to direct
operations and provide a lead in the chanting, which would be taken up
by all the people pulling on the ropes. As on Easter Island, the work was
accompanied by appropriate ceremony and feasting.

Huge stones have been transported, with only the most basic equipment, by many different peoples. In prehistoric Britain, the builders of
Stonehenge were part of a long established tradition of megalithic stone
transport. They stand out from the rest in the scale rather than the
nature of this particular branch of engineering. They transported more
stones than their predecessors, and the stones were generally larger and
brought from further afield.

The Egyptians probably had the greatest experience and the best
organization for this sort of work. The wall painting shows well orga-
nized and well directed teams who were probably used to the work.
Pouring a lubricant on the desert sand would seem to have been both
extravagant and pointless, and it may be that the sledge was pulled along

on a specially built roadway. According to Herodotus, the massive stones for the Great Pyramid were hauled along a roadway which took ten years to build. If the weight of the statue has been correctly estimated and if the painting gives an accurate representation of the work force, each man was pulling the equivalent of about 93 kg. In the French experiment, using rollers on a prepared track, each man was pulling a little over 160 kg.

Atkinson's schoolboys were pulling the equivalent of about 47 kg each. They were of course young, untrained for the work, and pulling uphill. Heyerdahl's Easter Island rabble were pulling the equivalent of about 67 kg each. They were a mixed team of men and women: everyone who could be assembled to take part. They, like Atkinson's team, were untrained and also did not have the advantage of a sledge. Furthermore the statue, once started, moved easily across the ground. The experiment did not test the minimum number of men required to pull a 12-tonne statue, but how easily a mixed gang of 180 people could move it, and the answer was 'very easily'. The number of people involved in the experiment was determined by the size of the available labour force, rather than any preconceived idea of the actual work-force required for the job. In Madagascar, the team of 300 people were pulling a mere 33 kg each. Taken at its face value, this seems relatively inefficient. But there is no suggestion that they were interested in the optimum work-force required to move a particular stone. The important thing was that the whole community should be involved in the work. Furthermore, 300 was the maximum number of people employed; perhaps for uphill stretches or over difficult terrain. Far fewer people may have been needed to pull such a stone where the going was good.

From the examples given above, it would seem that ten men per tonne (each pulling 100 kg) might be a reasonable average for hauling large stones over level ground, under favourable conditions or on specially prepared trackways. In wet weather, the work would quickly be brought to a halt, as the stones (with or without sledges) would tend to get bogged down. The heaviest stones at Stonehenge weigh about 50 tonnes and would thus probably have required a minimum of about five hundred men to haul them on level ground, and perhaps double that number for steep uphill stretches.

The work force is only one aspect of the cost of transporting the sarsen stones to Stonehenge. The other is time, and for this there is rather less evidence. The Egyptian wall painting is a silent witness and most of the experiments have been concerned with what can be achieved, rather than how long it would take. Atkinson, on the basis of his experiments, estimated a rate of progress of 0.8 km (half a mile) per day[7]. In Mohen's experiments with his model of a 32-tonne capstone, the rate of progress was slower, about 40 m (131 ft) in one morning. This is the largest stone on which such experiments have been conducted and was being pulled by fewer men per unit weight than the other stones. In Madagascar, a standing stone measuring more than 5 m (16½ ft) long by 80 cm (31 ins) wide by 1520 cm (6–8 ins) thick was erected to commemorate a royal marriage in 1797. This stone, which must have weighed about 2 tonnes, was quarried 30 km (19 miles) from the place where it was to be set up. Cutting the stone and transporting it took two months, during which time a hundred cattle were slaughtered.[8] Though we do not know how this time was divided, it is consistent with Atkinson's rate of 0.8 km (half a mile) a day.

As Atkinson pointed out, the steep escarpment of Redhorn Hill would have required considerable augmentation of the teams pulling stones southwards from the Marlborough Downs to Stonehenge. Possibly a supplementary team walked alongside, as in the Egyptian illustration, ready to provide necessary extra manpower for uphill stretches and relief at regular intervals on the level. A supplementary team of half the number required to haul a stone on level ground would probably be adequate for the uphill stretches and, on level ground, would ensure that each member of the team was relieved from duty for one out of every three stages of the journey. On this basis, about 750 men would have been involved in the transport of the largest (50 tonne) stones, and seventy-five men each for the much smaller (5 tonne) lintel stones. If 750 men had been employed throughout, all the sarsen stones for the circle and horseshoe could have been transported in about thirty-four journeys. Allowing nine weeks for the 77 km (48 mile) return journey to Stonehenge, this would mean that 750 men would take 306 weeks to drag all the sarsen stones to Stonehenge: that is nearly six years, without allowing any time off for bad weather or impossible ground conditions, or indeed for other essential activities such as harvesting. We have of

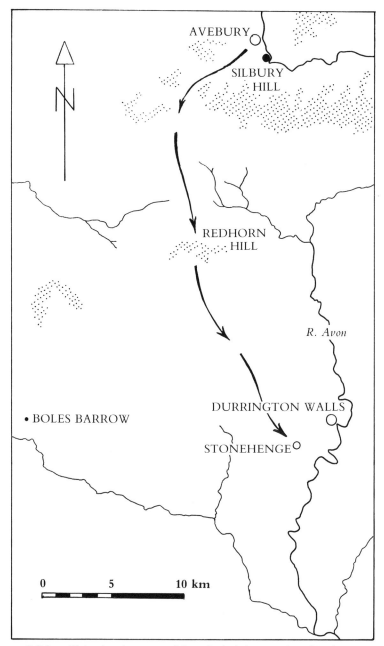

Salisbury Plain, showing some of the principal sites mentioned in the text
and the route (arrows) by which the sarsen stones may have been
transported to Stonehenge

course no means of knowing how many men (and maybe women) were employed on this work, but 750 is probably close to the minimum. With 1,500 men, the job could have been done in half the time taken by 750.

Shaping the stones

Apart from some preliminary splitting along joints, to bring the sarsen stones to roughly the right shape and size before transport, most of the dressing of the stones was done at Stonehenge. The need for splitting, to produce the shapes found at Stonehenge, is indicated by the quite different shapes found among the unworked stones of Avebury. The necessary splitting was probably achieved with the aid of fire, water, wedges and hammerstones.

The work done in shaping the stones of Stonehenge is quite without parallel in British stone circles. Other sites, such as the Ring of Brogar in Orkney, may give the impression of having carefully shaped stones, but this is because the Orkney sandstones split into much more regular shapes than the sarsens of Salisbury Plain. Evidence for the method of dressing the stones has been known since the time of Professor Gowland's 1901 excavation. He discovered large numbers of well used hammerstones and mauls in the packing of the stone holes round the base of the uprights. These stones are pebbles or boulders of sarsen, ranging from the size of a cricket ball up to that of a football, the largest weighing over 27 kg (60 lb). The position in which they were discovered, together with the fact that worked surfaces on sarsen uprights sometimes extend below ground level, shows that the dressing of the stones was done before they were erected.

The method of working is known in some detail because the best finish was generally only required on the inner faces of the uprights. On other surfaces, the shaping of the stones can be seen arrested at different stages. The coarsest shaping was done with the largest mauls and produced broad parallel grooves. Progressively finer work was done with smaller stones and produced finer grooves. Most of the work was done by repeated hammering, which reduced the rock to dust and gradually lowered the surface.[9] The heaviest mauls may have been wielded by several men using ropes. Every now and then the ridges between the resultant grooves were bashed away, producing the relatively small quantity of sarsen chips among the debris. Sarsen is a hard rock, one of the hardest, and it was a monumental task to try and reduce all these giants to more or less standard shapes. The final work was done by repeated pecking over the surface with a hammerstone and produced a finely pitted surface. This type of surface, well preserved below ground level, is identical to the surface of many axe hammers, and similar surfaces have been reproduced experimentally by pecking with a quartzite hammerstone.[10]

The builders of Stonehenge were not the first people in Britain to shape stones by hammering them. Quite apart from the roughly contemporary axe hammers and battle axes, many Neolithic stone axes had been shaped in this way. Similar pitted surfaces can be seen on many Cornish greenstone axes. What is remarkable about Stonehenge is the vast scale of the undertaking. Outside Britain, of course, there are many examples of monumental stone working – the great granite sculptures of Egypt and the Easter Island statues, for example.

There is a limited amount of experimental evidence, from which some idea can be formed of the labour costs involved in shaping the stones. E.H. Stone had some experiments carried out by a professional mason in 1923. The experiments indicated that pounding a sarsen stone with a heavy maul removed about 100 cm³ (6 in³) of sand and dust in an hour.[11] This is considerably faster than the rate for pecking battle axes and axe hammers,[12] but that is much finer work, with the implement held in one hand and the hammerstone in the other.

One of the most fascinating experiments was the attempt by Don Pedro Atan to carve a medium-sized, 4.5–6 m (15–20ft) long Easter Island statue at the request of Thor Heyerdahl. He decided he would need a team of six men for the job. After a nocturnal ritual of singing to the old god, Atua, they set out for the quarry on Rano Raraku. The mayor measured out the rock face, 'now by means of outstretched arms, now by spreading out his fingers'. Meanwhile his men had been gathering old abandoned stone picks, which lay around on the ledges in hundreds. Then, when the mayor had marked out the main points on the rock face, they started work:

They held their picks in their clenched hands like daggers, and at a sign from the mayor they burst into the stone-cutters' song . . . each

man lifting his arm and striking the rock face in time with the rhythm
of the tune. . . . It was so gripping and infectious that all of us who
saw it stood quite hypnotized.'[13]

At intervals they threw water at the rock, where they were pecking.
And, every now and then they would pick up a different pick, or stop to
sharpen the one they were using by means of a few sharp blows. A prehistoric technology was back in operation after a lapse of some three centuries. At the end of three days, the general form of the statue was clearly
taking shape in the rock face, but the men were tiring and the project was
abandoned. Calculations based on what they had already achieved suggested that it would take two teams of six men, working all day in shifts, about
a year to complete a medium-sized Easter Island statue

Quite apart from the quantitative archaeological value of this experiment, it provided a remarkable insight into the persistence of folk memory. When asked how he knew these things, the mayor replied that
when he was a small boy he used to sit at his grandfather's feet and learn
from him. He had to repeat everything until he was word perfect: all
the traditions, the genealogy, the customs, the songs. How long will
such memories last in the relatively literate twentieth century?

It is difficult to arrive at an estimate of the labour cost involved in
dressing the sarsen stones of Stonehenge. For a start, we have no means
of knowing how much stone was removed to bring them to their present
shape. On the basis of reasonable guesswork, E.H. Stone estimated a loss
of about 5m^3, from which it has been calculated that it would take a
team of fifty masons, working ten hours a day, seven days week, about
two years and nine months to shape the stones, excluding working the
mortices, tenons, tongues and grooves for the joints. The Easter Island
experiment is not easy to apply quantitatively to Stonehenge. Its
importance lies in the suggestion of other dimensions in the work of
stone dressing: the place of ritual in the preparation for such work, and
the importance of song and rhythm in its execution. More recent
examples of the association of song and rhythm with hard labour are our
own sea shanties.

Erecting the uprights

The sarsen uprights for Stonehenge III were lowered into their stone holes down ramps, sloping at an angle of about 45 degrees, and the opposite (vertical) face of the stone hole was protected from the impact by a row of wooden stakes. This much we know from the direct evidence of archaeological excavation. From this point on, we have to rely on the interpretation of experiments.

E.H. Stone, who was a retired engineer, carried out scale model experiments on the erection of the sarsen uprights at Stonehenge at one twelfth the natural scale.[14] Once the stone had been slid down the ramp, the engineers had to face the more difficult part of the job: raising it through a further 45 degrees to a vertical position. The only reasonable solution was to attach a rope (or ropes) round the top of the stone and pull it upright. This method would be very inefficient in terms of use of the available manpower, because the pull along the length of the rope would be at an acute angle to the length of the stone. More than half the work would thus be wasted, as far as rotating the stone about its base was concerned. Stone's solution was to set up a tall pair of shear legs behind the stone, so that the pull would come at a less acute angle to the length of the stone. Using this model, he showed that the pull needed to raise a sarsen upright weighing about 26 tonnes would be about 4.5 tonnes and this could be achieved by 180 men, each exerting a pull of 25 kg (56 lb).

There is no doubt that Stone's solution is correct according to his terms of reference. This would have been the most effective way of erecting the stones by pulling on ropes. But is it likely to have been the prehistoric solution to the problem? Blissfully unaware of such concepts as the triangle of forces, the Stonehenge engineer probably did not realize that most of the pull was being used up in a fruitless endeavour to drive the sarsen stone deeper into the ground. All he knew, and this was the accumulated wisdom of generations of stone raisers, was that pulling stones up into a vertical position was hard work, and if the stone could not be raised, more men would be needed on the ropes until it could.

Heyerdahl's series of experiments on Easter Island included the erection of a 25- to 30-tonne statue into its original position, standing upright on a stone platform. The whole operation was directed by Don

Pedro Atan, calling on the knowledge learned at the feet of his grand-father: knowledge of the science of engineering, passed down over three centuries without the benefit of a single practical exercise! The final stage of raising the statue to the vertical, from a slope of about 60 degrees, was achieved by a combination of leverage beneath its face and pulling on ropes tied round its head.[15]

Lying at an angle of 45 degrees along the ramp of its stone hole, the centre of gravity of the average upright in the sarsen circle would not be far above ground level. The stones are so wide that several levers could be set up side by side beneath them. A team of forty men using their full weight on 3.5 m poles would provide almost enough leverage to move a 26-tonne sarsen stone by themselves, without the aid of any pull on a rope. A combination of the use of levers and ropes, as on Easter Island, would have been very effective. The number of men needed for the job would depend on the length of the poles used for levers and the length of the ropes (and hence the angle between the rope and the length of the stone). The Easter Island statue was rocked from its 60-degree slope to the vertical in one move. If this could not be achieved from a 45-degree slope with a large sarsen stone, the necessary move-ment could be made in stages, each of which could be consolidated by inserting hammerstones and mauls between the stone and the underlying ramp. The total labour force required would probably be considerably less than half the 180 estimated by Stone for his method of pulling the stone up from behind, even with the aid of shear legs.

Raising the lintels

Two methods have been proposed for raising the lintels so that they could be set on top of the uprights. One is by constructing sloping ramps and hauling the stones up the ramps: a method also supposed to have been used in building the pyramids of Egypt. The other is by rais-ing them vertically in small stages with the aid of levers. There are sev-eral serious objections to the ramp theory. Atkinson pointed out that there was no archaeological evidence for the former presence of such ramps, nor for the quarry from which the 300 m³ (at least 10,000 ft³) of material might have been dug. He also commented on the colossal amount of labour involved in dismantling and remaking the ramp for each lintel to be raised. Also the ramp would have to extend far enough beyond the uprights to accommodate enough men to haul a 5-tonne lintel up the prepared slope.

The alternative and more likely method makes use of levers. One end of the stone to be lifted is raised by means of levers and a short piece of timber inserted beneath it. The other end is then raised in the same way. As the stone is raised, a timber framework is built up around it and beneath it, until the stone has been lifted vertically to the required height.[16] This method was successfully employed by Mohen in the French experiments with a 32-tonne concrete capstone. Herodotus, writing in the fifth century BC, suggests that a similar method was used in building the Egyptian pyramids some 2,000 years earlier:

> The method employed was to build it in steps, or, as some call them, tiers or terraces. When the base was complete, the blocks for the first tier above it were lifted from ground level by contrivances made of short timbers; on this first tier there was another which raised them higher still. Each tier, or storey, had its set of levers, or it may be that they used the same one, which, being easy to carry, they shifted up from stage to stage as soon as its load was dropped into place. Both methods are mentioned, so I give them both here.[17]

Once again the Easter Islanders, with their folk memory stretching back over 300 years, provided a splendid practical demonstration of megalithic engineering in action. The problem they faced was raising a statue weighing 25 to 30 tonnes up on to the stone platform off which it had been tipped during the statue-overthrowing-time. The statue lay face down on the ground below the platform. Maintaining its recumbent posture, the statue was first raised vertically to a height of about 3.5 m (12 ft) above ground level (just what was required for the Stonehenge lintel stones) and then finally tilted till it came to rest standing on the platform. It took twelve men ten days to raise this 25- to 30-tonne statue to a height of 3.5 m (12 ft) above ground level. Most of the time they worked with two levers, each operated by five men. The mayor, Don Pedro Atan was directing the operation and his younger brother was placing stones (gathered from the nearby beach) beneath the

Easter Island statue being raised on a growing pile of boulders
from the beach

statue each time one side was raised a little by the levers. By the end, the men working on the levers were dangling from them on ropes, as they were so far above the ground. Heyerdahl gives a graphic account of the whole process, as well as the nocturnal ceremony of song and dance the night before they started work.[18] The sarsen stone lintels for the outer circle can be no more than a fifth of the weight of the Easter Island statue and the problem of raising them therefore correspondingly less.

Conclusions

The cost of Stonehenge III, in terms of human labour and time, has been widely appreciated, particularly since the publication of Atkinson's book. The sarsen circle and horseshoe must have been designed and laid out on the ground at the same time, and then built while the design was still clear. Herodotus tells us that it took twenty years to build the Great

Pyramid, but we must probably allow considerably less than this for the design and completion of Stonehenge III.

So what was the cost of building Stonehenge III? Hauling the stones 38.5 km (24 miles), from near Avebury to Stonehenge, represents, on anyone's reckoning, by far the greatest component of the labour cost in the whole undertaking. A minimum of 750 men must have worked for at least six years, probably nearer nine years, if we make a reasonable allowance for time lost due to unfavourable conditions and time off for gathering the harvests. In the same period of time, fifty or more masons could have completed all the dressing of the stones as they arrived. Once all the stones were on site and satisfactorily shaped, there would have been so much labour available, that the work of erecting the uprights and raising the lintels could have been completed in a matter of weeks. From conception to completion, the sarsen circle and horseshoe could have been built in nine years, using a labour force of no more than about 800 men. Such a time-scale makes sense in terms of the reasonable life expectancy of the man behind its design. It has already been suggested in an earlier chapter that he may have died before he was able to complete the bluestone part of his design.

Bluestone lintel freshly excavated

The real cost of Stonehenge III is difficult to express in a meaningful way. Expressed in late twentieth-century British terms, it might be around £50,000,000. In late eighteenth-century Madagascan terms, it might be represented by the slaughter of 100,000 cattle. In British Bronze Age terms, it might have occupied the entire adult male population of an area of, at the very least, 260 km² (100 square miles) for six to nine years. However we express it, it was an astonishing achievement and a sure indication of just how far these people had advanced beyond mere subsistence. This must have been an age of peace and plenty, an age of political stability, a golden age, contrasting in almost every respect with the supposed 'Age of Arthur' in the fifth and sixth centuries AD.

The skill of the builders of Stonehenge III was a source of amazement to Henry of Huntingdon nearly eight centuries ago and is still a source of wonder today. It gives the impression that they must have had some secret knowledge which has long since been lost. In fact this does not seem to have been the case. They almost certainly had knowledge of the simplest of all machines, the lever, and probably also appreciated the

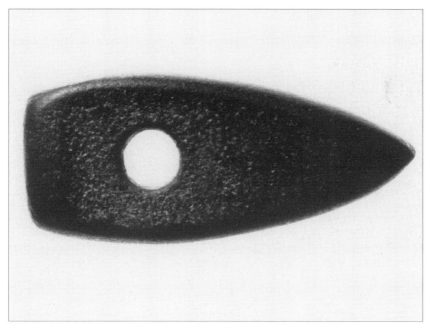

Dolerite (Group XVIII) axe hammer from Lincolnshire

use of sledges for transporting heavy loads. Beyond this, they applied a basic qualitative principle of simple proportion. If you can't pull a load with fifty men, try sixty, seventy, a hundred, or a hundred and fifty. If you can shape a piece of stone into an axe or battle axe by pecking away at it with a hammerstone, then you can do the same to a gigantic block of sarsen stone. It will just take a lot longer. Indeed, Stonehenge might aptly be described as a monument to simple proportion.

If Stonehenge was not the product of a scientific or technical break-through, then what does this totally unique and quite extraordinary building represent? The answer must be that it represents a quite un-precedented administrative achievement. The organization of such a large body of men, coordinating their activities over such distances, on such diverse tasks, and for such a long time, tells us more about society than about science. It tells us of men of vision, men with ambitions, and men with the power and ability to fulfil them.

CHAPTER 11

THE TEMPLE OF AMBRIUS: RELIGION AT STONEHENGE

Stonehenge is the one essential clue, that Geoffrey of Monmouth provided, to finding a place for King Arthur in prehistory. But it is also much more than that. In the absence of contemporary written records, it is itself the most eloquent voice to reach us from that distant prehistoric 'Age of Arthur'. Already, in considering the cost of building Stonehenge III, we have been able to form some idea of the general character of the age. It was a period of political and economic stability, of strong government and efficient administration, most likely under the influence of a powerful ruling dynasty. There can be little doubt that Stonehenge was built to impress. Visitors, whether from far or near, must have gazed in wonder at the grandeur of the design, the size of the stones, the curvature of the lintels, the beauty of the setting. For those who saw it, it must surely have been one of the wonders of the known world. And if the building was wonderful, so also was the king at whose command it was built. It must have given the people a tremendous feeling of national pride, like the Temple of Solomon in Jerusalem, which took seven years to build and is described in such minute detail in the First Book of Kings.[1]

The Temple of Solomon. The name of the king was linked to the great temple he built, and the connection has long outlasted the building itself, which has been destroyed and rebuilt many times since. Stonehenge III: the Temple of Ambrius. Was this also named after the king who built it? According to Geoffrey of Monmouth, Stonehenge was built at the command of King Aurelius Ambrosius, the Ambrosius of Nennius and Ambrosius Aurelianus of Gildas. Geoffrey also tells us, when describing the first visit of this king to the Cloister of Ambrius, that 'it was Ambrius, so they say, who had founded the monastery years before'.[2] Ambrosius and Ambrius are simply different Latin forms of the

British (Welsh) name, Emrys. Geoffrey, without realizing it, is giving us the same piece of information twice: that Stonehenge, the prehistoric Temple of Ambrius, was built by order of King Ambrius. This is a fair indication that the tradition was an ancient one.

Ambrosius Aurelianus, the historical leader of the British resistance to the Saxon invaders, may have started life as Aurelius and acquired the name Ambrosius in recognition of his victorious campaigns. Whatever the explanation, the names and the stories had become thoroughly confused by the time Geoffrey collected them and set them down in his history. It is quite possible that Amesbury, known as Ambresbyrig in the ninth century AD,[3] took its name from the nearby Temple of Ambrius, rather than from the post-Roman British leader Ambrosius Aurelianus.

Geoffrey, who preserved the names of Ambrius and Merlin for us, has nothing at all to say about the god to whom the temple they built was dedicated. For him, it had become medievalized as the Cloister of Ambrius, 'a monastery of three hundred brethren'. Diodorus, writing more than a thousand years earlier and retelling what was already ancient history in his time, may be nearer the mark. But does the building itself shed any light on its own function? Was it for example, as some have claimed, an astronomical observatory?

The idea that Stonehenge might have been an astronomical observatory owes much to the work of G.S. Hawkins, Professor of Astronomy at the University of Boston.[4] He found that there were many lines at Stonehenge, either between pairs of stones or through pairs of archways, which pointed towards the rising or setting of the sun or full moon, either at midsummer or midwinter, at a date of 1500 BC. But, as Hawkins himself admitted:

> I cannot prove beyond all doubt that Stonehenge was used as an astronomical observatory. A time machine would be needed to prove that. Although the stones line up with dozens of important Sun and Moon positions the builders of Stonehenge might somehow have remained in ignorance of the fact.[5]

The problem is to determine whether or not the astronomical directions built into Stonehenge are statistically significant or not. This is a difficult question and we have certainly not heard the end of it, though current thinking is that the lines are not far removed from what one might expect by chance.[6] As far as Stonehenge III is concerned, the lines in question pass through the trilithon archways and out through wider archways in the sarsen circle. But there are so many such lines coming through the archways of the sarsen circle that no statistics are needed to see that there is nothing remarkable about these astronomical lines.

When Stonehenge was complete, anyone standing in the central area would have had a very real feeling of being inside a building, open to the sky it is true, but very much closed in from the country outside. The sarsen uprights in the outer circle are about twice the width of the gaps between them, so the 'window space' is about one-third of the full circle. Of this space, about two-fifths would have been blocked by the massive uprights of the sarsen trilithons, bringing the window space down to no more than one-fifth of the full circle. This is about the same ratio of window to wall as in the great circular Roman Catholic Cathedral of Liverpool. In both buildings, shafts of light, streaming in through narrow vertical windows, illuminate the central area and give it life. This is brilliant architecture for a temple, but, with eighty per cent of the horizon permanently blocked from view, the design could hardly have been worse for observing the rising and setting of the heavenly bodies.

There is just one astronomical line at Stonehenge on which everyone is agreed, and that is the axis, the line passing from the centre of the circle out through the entrance and along the avenue. This direction, which received special attention in one way or another at every stage in the development of Stonehenge, points towards the midsummer sunrise. This fact suggests that sun worship was important at Stonehenge and that the summer solstice was an important religious festival. It is however worth pointing out that the east-west orientation of most churches might also be taken as an indication of sun worship, with special festivals at the equinoxes.

Apart from astronomical lines built into Stonehenge, there is one particular stone which may have some significance in this context, and that is the Altar Stone. As far as Stonehenge is concerned, this stone is unique. It is neither a sarsen stone nor a bluestone; neither local to Wessex nor brought from Mynydd Preselau. It is the largest of the foreign stones and, though now fallen, must have occupied a special place at Stonehenge. Since it was so clearly an important stone, and yet did not come from the sacred mountain, it was presumably brought to Stonehenge because it possessed some special properties. What was so special about this stone?

The Altar Stone is a fine-grained micaceous sandstone. The mica flakes all lie more or less parallel to the stratification, thus enabling the rock to split fairly readily in this direction. Mica is a shiny mineral, having what is described as a pearly lustre. Sunlight shining on the surface of such a rock is reflected by literally thousands of tiny mica mirrors and, since these are all roughly parallel, the whole surface of the rock becomes a sort of compound mirror, too rough to see your face in but good enough to reflect the light of the sun brilliantly. The Altar Stone is thought to have stood on the axis of Stonehenge, inside the bluestone horseshoe and a little to the southwest of the centre. It is 1 m (3 ft 6 in) wide and 0.5 m (1 ft 9 in) thick. The stones of Stonehenge III are arranged tangentially in relation to the curves (circles or horseshoes) on which they stand. On this basis, the Altar Stone would have stood with its width across the axis. In this orientation, the micaceous planes of stratification must have faced north-eastwards and south-westwards along the axis of Stonehenge. When the midsummer sun rose and shone through the entrance, its light would have been reflected straight back from the surface of the Altar Stone. A similar reflection of the last rays of the setting sun at midwinter would have been blocked by Stone 67 of the bluestone horseshoe.

A single stone with strong reflecting properties, brought specially to Stonehenge, independently of all the other stones, and set up in a prominent axial position so that the sun's rays were reflected back towards their source at midsummer: this does not seem like chance. At midsummer the Stonehenge people would have been enjoying the full benefits of the warmth and light derived from the sun. Setting up a special stone to reflect some of this light straight back to its source at such a time could be interpreted as a token sacrifice to the sun god. At the very least, it adds to the impression that Stonehenge was a temple to the sun.

Two further features in the design of Stonehenge may have some ritual, religious or functional significance. One is the distribution of floor space and the other the height of the trilithons.

The radius of the sarsen circle is only about one-third the radius of the surrounding bank. This circle thus encloses about one-ninth of the total area in the Stonehenge enclosure. Within this area, the available space is further restricted by the presence of the giant sarsen trilithon horseshoe and the bluestone circle and horseshoe. It follows that, despite the grandeur of Stonehenge III and the size of the population for which it must have been the religious centre, the number of people who could actually assemble inside it at any one time was severely restricted. The implication of this seems to be quite simple. At great festivals, the priests performed the mysteries connected with their religion inside the sarsen circle, unseen by the people outside. This suggested division is similar to that between choir and nave in medieval cathedrals and abbeys. The area between the sarsen circle and the enclosing bank, and indeed out beyond the bank, would have been ideal for the people to dance, probably clockwise (or, in Stonehenge terms, sunwise, moonwise or starwise), round the central stones.

As Atkinson has remarked about the trilithons, 'there seems no doubt that the builders were anxious to display above ground the maximum height of stone that was compatible with apparent stability and safety'.[7] This is a curious feature of the building, because, though the trilithons are superb structures in themselves, they actually detract from the perfection of the lintelled sarsen stone circle, the structural basis of the 'spherical temple'. It seems likely that there must have been some good reason for erecting these massive trilithons inside the circle. What is so special about the height of the trilithons? One possibility is that they provided high platforms in an area totally devoid of natural rocky eminences. It is difficult for any leader, religious or secular, to be seen by the people or heard by the people, when they are all on the same level ground. Even today, in this age of television, the Royal Family appears before the people on great state occasions, high above the crowd, on the balcony of Buckingham Palace. Every day at noon, the Pope appears in a window of his apartment overlooking St Peter's Square and says the Angelus with the assembled pilgrims. Those who have no such high station in life, but still wish to communicate with the people, carry their own personal soap-box to Speakers' Corner in Hyde Park, or wherever else they may have chosen to meet their public. The need for a platform is common to all those who, for whatever reason, wish to appear before the public.

So much for the silent witness of the stones themselves. For literary clues, we turn first to Diodorus, for whose legends about the Hyperboreans we have developed a certain respect. He has this to say about the religion of the Hyperboreans:

> Leto was born on this island, and for that reason Apollo is honoured among them above all other gods, and the inhabitants are looked upon as priests of Apollo, after a manner, since daily they praise this god continuously in song and honour him exceedingly. And there is also on the island both a magnificent sacred precinct of Apollo and a notable temple which is adorned with many votive offerings and is spherical in shape. Furthermore a city is there which is sacred to this god, and the majority of its inhabitants are players on the cithara; and these continually play on this instrument in the temple and sing hymns of praise to the god, glorifying his deeds.[8]

To suggest that we follow Diodorus to the extent of believing that Stonehenge was a temple to the Greek god Apollo would be stretching our credulity beyond its breaking point. But it would also be taking Diodorus much too literally. The Greeks tended, where appropriate, to identify the gods of other peoples with their own. Thus Imhotep, who had been deified by the sixth century BC, was identified with Asclepios, the Greek god of healing, and the greatest of all the temples built in his honour was known by the Greeks as the Asclepieion. Diodorus took his account of the Hyperboreans from the writings of Hecataeus, dating from about 500 BC, by which time Apollo was becoming identified with the oriental sun gods. If the religion of the Hyperboreans was actually directed towards the sun, it would be perfectly natural for Hecataeus to claim that they honoured Apollo above all other gods. This suggestion is consistent with the general interest that the Hyperboreans seem to have taken in astronomy.

> They also say that the moon, as viewed from this island, appears to be but a little distance from the earth and to have upon it prominences, like those of the earth, which are visible to the eye. The account is also given that the god visits the island every nineteen years, the period in which the return of the stars to the same place in the heavens is

accomplished; and for this reason the nineteen-year period is called by
the Greeks the 'year of Meton'. At the time of this appearance of the
god, he both plays on the cithara and dances continuously the night
through from the vernal equinox until the rising of the Pleiades,
expressing in this manner his delight in his successes.[8]

The statement about the proximity of the moon to the earth is a perfectly reasonable and correct deduction from observation. The moon
travels the full circuit of the zodiac every month and its motion against
the background of the stars is therefore sufficiently rapid to be detectable
even in a single night's observation. Furthermore permanent surface features are visible on the face of the moon and these must somehow have
been correctly interpreted by the Hyperboreans as topographic features,
similar to those on the earth. Both these observations would lead to the
conclusion that the moon is relatively close to the earth compared with
all the other heavenly bodies.

The nineteen-yearly visit of the god to the island has aroused a great
deal of interest. R.S. Newall, in his letter to Hawkins about Diodorus,
asked: 'Could the full moon do something spectacular once every nineteen years at Stonehenge?'[9] Hawkins took up the challenge of this question with enthusiasm and soon came up with the 18.61-year cycle of
regression of the lunar nodes.[10] He showed how, with the aid of the
fifty-six Aubrey Holes and observations of the sun and moon across certain stone alignments, this cycle could have been used at Stonehenge to
predict solar and lunar eclipses; fifty-six years being a close approxima-
tion to three 18.61-year cycles. While it remains true that the Aubrey
Holes could have been used as Hawkins suggested, or in related ways
that have been proposed subsequently,[11] it seems rather unlikely that they
actually were so used. They were dug very early in the long history of
Stonehenge and were almost immediately back-filled. By the time the
Station Stones (Hawkins's most important astronomical markers) were
erected, the Aubrey Holes would have been no more than shallow, turf
covered hollows, whose very existence may well have been quite
unknown.

The alternative view would be that the Hyperboreans had themselves
discovered the Metonic cycle, as implied by Diodorus. The appearance
of the god apparently took place at the vernal equinox, so Newall's

question should perhaps be rephrased as follows: 'Could the full moon do something spectacular once every nineteen years *at the vernal equinox?*' The answer is quite clearly 'Yes'. In the fifth century BC, the Greek astronomer Meton discovered that 235 lunar months are equal to nineteen solar years, so that after one Metonic cycle of nineteen years, the full moon occurs again on the same calendar date. The vernal equinox is just such a calendar date and, on that date, once every nineteen years, the full moon sets in the west as the sun is rising in the east. Such was the occasion for the visit of the god to the island of the Hyperboreans.

Apart from the fact that this is what Diodorus tells us, is it likely that the Hyperboreans could have discovered the nineteen-year Metonic cycle over a thousand years before the Greek astronomer after whom it is named? The first point to note, in answer to this question, is that this is much more likely than the discovery of the 18.61- or fifty-six year cycle of regression of the lunar nodes, simply because of the limited life expectancy of an individual prehistoric astronomer, philosopher or priest. Secondly, they may have discovered the nineteen-year cycle without having appreciated, as Meton did, that it was equivalent to 235 lunar months.

The sun and moon both provide a basis for recording the passage of time, in years and months respectively, but unfortunately there is not an exact number of lunar months in the solar year. This problem is well illustrated by the Christian religious festivals of Christmas and Easter. The date of Christmas, in the absence of any historical information about the date of birth of Jesus, follows the pagan festival of midwinter, the 'birthday' of the sun, and occupies a fixed place in the solar calendar. The date of Easter, on the other hand, is determined by historical events which are recorded as having taken place at the time of the Passover. This ancient Jewish religious festival was observed on the night of the full moon nearest to the vernal equinox. Easter is thus fixed in relation to a lunar calendar, and that is why it moves around the months of March and April in such a seemingly random manner. If the Hyperboreans, as is quite likely, celebrated both solar (equinox and solstice) and lunar (full moon) festivals, they would have found that, every nineteen years, these would fall on the same days and such days might well have provided an excuse for mega-festivals, occasions marked by special visitations of their god; and when the god danced through the night, the people would surely have danced with him.

For details of early Apollo worship at Delos, which may have some bearing on the religious observances of the Hyperboreans at Stonehenge, we turn again to Homer, and his 'Hymn to Delian Apollo':

Yet in Delos do you most delight your heart; for there the long-robed Ionians gather in your honour with their children and shy wives. Mindful, they delight you with boxing and dancing and song, so often as they hold their gathering. . .

. . . And there is this great wonder besides – and its renown shall never perish – the girls of Delos, hand-maidens of the Far-shooter: for when they have praised Apollo first, and also Leto and Artemis who delights in arrows, they sing a strain telling of men and women of past days, and charm the tribes of men. Also they can imitate the tongues of all men and their clattering speech: each would say that he himself were singing, so close to the truth is their sweet song.[12]

This sounds remarkably like an early example of the phenomenon known as speaking in tongues, which is recorded in the Acts of the Apostles[13] and discussed by Saint Paul, in his first letter to the Corinthians.[14] Did the Delians learn this from the Hyperboreans? If so, it might explain why the Delians persuaded the Hyperborean women to stay in Delos, why their tombs occupied such a prominent position in the Temple of Artemis, and why they were still honoured in the time of Herodotus, more than a thousand years after their death. Further information about the cult of Apollo is given by Homer in his 'Hymn to Pythean Apollo'. Apollo, having chosen the site for his temple at Delphi, beneath Mount Parnassus, announced his plans:

In this place I am minded to build a glorious temple to be an oracle for men, and here they will always bring perfect hecatombs, both they who dwell in rich Peleponnesus and the men of Europe and from all the wave-washed isles, coming to question me. And I will deliver to them all counsel that cannot fail, answering them in my rich temple.[15]

As in the 'Hymn to Delian Apollo', the bringing of hecatombs (originally a sacrifice of a hundred oxen) and the richness of the temple are stressed. The important function of this temple was to be an oracle, where people could come and consult Apollo himself, through a human medium. Further on, in the same hymn, Homer tells how Apollo selected the first ministers to serve him in his new temple. He waylaid some Cretan merchants from Cnossos and persuaded them to leave their ship and follow him. When they reached the temple, the Cretans looked around them and wondered how they would be able to survive in such a barren environment, quite apart from carrying out their duties in the temple. But Apollo hastened to reassure them:

Foolish mortals and poor drudges are you, that you seek cares and hard toils and straits. Easily will I tell you a word and set it in your hearts. Though each one of you with knife in hand should slaughter sheep continually, yet would you always have abundant store, even all that the glorious tribes of men bring here for me. But guard you my temple and receive the tribes of men that gather at this place, and especially show mortal men my will, and do you always keep right-eousness in your heart.[16]

Geoffrey of Monmouth has little to add to this aspect of the study of Stonehenge, as his account is written in the context of Christianity. However Merlin, who masterminded the building of Stonehenge for Aurelius, is introduced as an oracular figure who amazed Vortigern by his prophecies. By the time he was brought to Aurelius to discuss the plans for building Stonehenge, his powers were well known:

The King received Merlin gaily and ordered him to prophesy the future, for he wanted to hear some marvels from him. 'Mysteries of that sort cannot be revealed, except where there is the most urgent need for them. If I were to utter them as an entertainment, or where there was no need at all, then the spirit which controls me would for-sake me in the moment of need.'[17]

At this stage it is worth returning to the confusion over Merlin's name: Merlin who, as Geoffrey tells us, was also called Ambrosius. This has its origin in the story about Vortigern and the fatherless boy prophet, as told by Nennius. When Vortigern's wizards had been thoroughly confounded, the boy prophet (who had not been named) proceeded to interpret the battle between the red dragon and the white dragon:

'This mystery is revealed to me, and I will make it plain to you. The cloth represents your kingdom, and the two worms are two dragons. The red worm is your dragon, and the lake represents the world. But the white one is the dragon of the people who have seized many peoples and countries in Britain, and will reach almost from sea to sea; but later our people will arise, and will valiantly throw the English people across the sea. But do you go forth from this fortress, for you cannot build it, and travel over many provinces, to find a safe fortress, and I will stay here.' Then the king asked the lad 'What is your name?' He replied 'I am called Ambrosius.'[18]

In Geoffrey's account of this story, when Vortigern asked Merlin to interpret the battle between the dragons:

Merlin immediately burst into tears. He went into a prophetic trance and then spoke as follows: 'Alas for the Red Dragon, for its end is near. Its cavernous dens shall be occupied by the White Dragon, which stands for the Saxons whom you have invited over. The Red Dragon represents the people of Britain, who will be overrun by the White One: for Britain's mountains and valleys shall be levelled, and the streams in its valleys shall run with blood.'[19]

Vortigern, in this part of the story, is clearly consulting an oracle. It is quite possible that this is the oldest part of the tradition, with Merlin's 'virgin birth' and his dispute with Vortigern's wizards added later, perhaps, as was suggested in an earlier chapter, in response to the spread of Christianity. Vortigern was probably well aware that these mysteries were being revealed, not by Merlin himself, but by some spirit speaking through his mediumship. What he wanted to know was the ultimate authority for the dread pronouncements which were being presented to him; and the answer came back, 'I am called Ambrosius.' Ambrosius (Ambrius), the king who had ordered the building of Stonehenge, the king who had established the supremacy of the dynasty which Vortigern had brought to ruin: that was the voice that brought him so little comfort in his hour of desperate need.

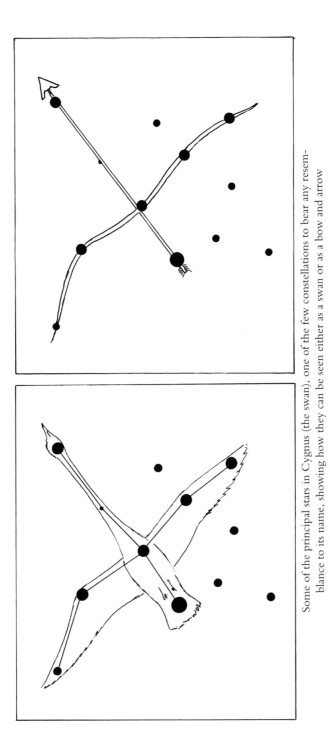

Some of the principal stars in Cygnus (the swan), one of the few constellations to bear any resemblance to its name, showing how they can be seen either as a swan or as a bow and arrow

The confusion of names is more apparent than real and, once the oracular nature of Merlin's prophecy is appreciated, it disappears altogether. Nennius suppressed the name Merlin, in an attempt to identify the Ambrosius of the prophecy with Ambrosius, the successful fifth-century British military leader. Geoffrey, who uses the name Merlin throughout, adds the fact that he was sometimes called Ambrosius, but only in this particular context.

Diodorus, unfortunately, makes no mention of Merlin, Ambrius or Arthur. He does, however, introduce another Hyperborean called Abaris, who 'came to Greece in ancient times and renewed the goodwill and kinship of his people to the Delians'.[20] The legend of Abaris seems to have been of considerable antiquity several centuries earlier, when Herodotus wrote: 'As for the tale of Abaris, who is said to have been a Hyperborean, and to have gone with his arrow all round the world without once eating, I shall pass it by in silence.'[21] From what Herodotus did say, Abaris seems more like a god than a human Hyperborean, and the fact that he carried an arrow on his journey round the world is reminiscent of Apollo. An unceasing journey round the world suggests an astronomical connection, possibly an important constellation. The constellation of Cygnus (the swan), which does bear some resemblance to a swan in flight, could equally well be interpreted as a bow and arrow. If this interpretation is accepted, then the head of the archer can be seen in Cepheus, the elbow of the arm drawing the bow in Cassiopeia, and the legs in Pegasus. The whole of this compound constellation might have been known as Abaris to the Hyperboreans. We cannot possibly know for sure, and this must remain pure speculation. But with their eyes and minds directed to the heavens, the Hyperboreans must have devised some system for ordering the multitude of the stars into manageable constellations that could be recognized and known, and it is inherently unlikely that they would have devised the same system as the Greeks.

CHAPTER 12

EGYPTIAN ANALOGY: PREHISTORIC CIVILIZATION IN BRITAIN?

Great architecture, and Stonehenge has a good claim to be considered in this category, has generally been associated with civilization. The concept of civilization, however, seems so foreign to British prehistory that it would hardly merit discussion, were it not for the unique character of Stonehenge itself and the associated Wessex Culture. Something big was happening on Salisbury Plain at the turn of the millenium, round about 2000 BC. To use an expression often trivialized today, history was being made. But since there was no one there with pen and paper to record the fact, the memory of it has almost completely disappeared in the great encircling morass of prehistory.

The people of this latest and greatest period of Stonehenge boasted a rich aristocracy, a powerful and efficient administration, a well established religion and priesthood, a sound empirical knowledge of all the major branches of science, and a network of communications on a national and international scale. All these things they shared with the great civilizations of Egypt, the eastern Mediterranean, the Middle East and the Indus Valley. But the very word civilization implies something more. It implies the existence of cities and it is here that the comparison seems to break down. There are no cities of this period on Salisbury Plain. No city . . . no civilization!

But Diodorus assures us that there was a city, that it was sacred to the god Apollo, and that 'the majority of its inhabitants are players on the cithara and continually play on this instrument in the temple.'[1] As far as the Greeks were concerned, there was a city and it was at no great distance from the temple. The Delians had exchanged visits with the Hyperboreans. They had been there. Is it possible then that there was indeed a city near Stonehenge, which has left so little trace that it has entirely escaped detection? In spite of his own rather dismissive view of them, the legends of the Hyperboreans recorded by Diodorus have generally proved reliable, wherever they can be tested.

The cities of the Middle East and the Indus Valley were largely constructed of mud bricks. In the course of time, mud brick buildings decay and have to be replaced. Thus, over the centuries, the resultant accumulation of inorganic debris assumes topographic proportions. The tels of the Middle East are prominent landmarks and, when excavated, reveal a complex structural history of the growth and development of ancient cities. Other cities, in the eastern Mediterranean region for example, were built of stone and their ruins have withstood the ravages of time. Nearer home are the Neolithic villages of Orkney, where the local sandstone provided a building material of such superb quality that the neolithic houses and chambered tombs are unsurpassed anywhere in Western Europe. But on Salisbury Plain there was no good building stone and the climate was totally unsuited to the production of sun-baked mud bricks. The main building material would undoubtedly have been timber and, in the long term, timber buildings are biodegradable. Wood is an organic material. It is a source of food for various wood boring insects or their larvae. It provides a substratum for wood-rotting fungi and other plants. Nothing is wasted. Nothing is left. Timber buildings decay without trace . . . well, almost.

Anyone in the least acquainted with archaeological excavation will be aware that, although the timbers themselves may have disappeared completely, the post-holes in which they were set in the ground remain distinct from the surrounding sub-soil. Post-holes are particularly easy to recognize in chalk, as their soft dark filling shows up in such marked contrast to the solid white of the natural chalk. Nor is the contrast restricted to physical appearance. In certain conditions, particularly drought, the relatively deep soil of the post holes supports a better growth of grass or cereal than the thin soil overlying the adjacent chalk. Such crop marks may even be detected from the air, as in the classic case of Woodhenge, 3 km (a little under two miles) east of Stonehenge. This famous site was totally unknown until it was observed and photographed from the air by Squadron Leader G.S.M. Insall VC, in 1925.

The most likely site for the city of Diodorus's account is the great banked enclosure of Durrington Walls, about two miles north-east of Stonehenge. This site has yielded radiocarbon dates in the range 2500 to 2000 BC, rather earlier than the Wessex Culture – Stonehenge III period. It is widely considered to have been a tribal centre or capital. It has been interpreted as a village of some two hundred inhabitants,[2] as a town with a population of between 1,200 and 1,800 people,[3] and as a centre for meetings, rallies, fairs, markets, festivals and other entertainments required by a scattered society.[4] The uncertainty is due to the problem of interpreting the evidence of very limited excavation. Two round buildings have been excavated, the larger of the two having a diameter of 23 m (75 ft), three more are detectable on aerial photographs, and others are suggested by geophysical surveys.

Five round houses in a circular enclosure hardly constitute a city, but many more buildings may remain undetected by aerial photography and even undetectable by excavation. One of the intriguing findings of the excavations at Stonehenge was that the surface of the natural chalk under the highest part of the bank was about 30 cm (1 ft) higher than in adjacent areas. It was as if the artificial bank had followed the line of an earlier natural ridge in the chalk. This curious phenomenon was explained by Atkinson as being due to the gradual lowering of the chalk surface by the solvent action of acid rain water.[5] Under the bank, the natural chalk was (at least in part) protected against solution by the overlying chalk rubble. Post-holes of this age can thus only be discovered if the original post penetrated more than about 30 cm into the chalk. It is unlikely that the average domestic building needed its supporting timbers to be sunk deeper than 30 cm into the underlying chalk.

Durrington Walls is generally classed as a henge, but among such monuments it is one of a small group of giants, mostly situated on Salisbury Plain. With a diameter of a little over 470 m (1500 ft), however, it still seems a bit on the small side for a city. But, in this connection, we must keep a sense of proportion. The great city of Troy, also well known to the Greeks, is actually very little larger than Durrington Walls. As far as its size goes, this city of the Hyperboreans just about makes the grade for its particular period of history.

Stonehenge may not classify as great architecture on a world scale, nor the Wessex Culture as a great civilization. Their extent, both in space and time was too small. But the Wessex Culture–Stonehenge III phenomenon bears such similarities to civilization, that it may be worth pursuing the analogy. The rise and fall of the great civilizations of the world is the theme of Professor Arnold Toynbee's great work, *A Study of History*.[6] Toynbee identified twenty-one civilizations in the history of the world, of which all but six were affiliated in some way to earlier civilizations. Our own Western civilization, for example, is affiliated to the earlier Hellenic civilization, which included the Roman Empire. The six primary civilizations recognized by Toynbee are the Egyptiac, the Minoan, the Sumeric, the Sinic, the Andean and the Mayan.

The growth of a civilization, in Toynbee's analysis, depends on the interplay of two main factors: challenge and response. The challenge is presented by the environment (the physical environment in the case of the primary civilizations); the response is the physical and mental effort employed by the people in meeting this environmental challenge. An unchallenging environment, an idyllic land of plenty, requires only minimal response. Such an environment, though seeming to provide the necessary leisure for the development of society, fails to provide the stimulus. A more difficult environment demands qualities of determination, resourcefulness and inventiveness from its human inhabitants, without which they will fail to survive. By the time the environment is finally brought under control, these human qualities are well established and men of drive and ambition turn their attention to new outlets for their energies. Civilization is in the making. Examples of environmental challenges which have led to civilizations are marshes, jungle and flood waters (Egyptiac and Sumeric); the sea (Minoan); tropical rain-forest (Mayan); bleak plateau and poor soil (Andean). There are, however, some environments which are so severe that mere human survival requires almost total commitment and there is little spare energy for further development. Examples of such environments, and the 'arrested civilizations' to which they gave rise are Arctic shores (Eskimo); oceanic islands (Polynesian); the Steppe (Nomad).

The challenge of drought has been a familiar and distressing sight on our television screens in recent years. There is nothing new in this challenge. During the last Ice Age, the area now occupied by the deserts of the northern Sahara and Arabia was pleasant grassland with a rich and varied fauna, an environment in which the human species flourished. As the northern ice sheets retreated, other climatic belts followed in their wake. The rains, which had watered the grasslands of North Africa and Arabia during the Ice Age, gradually deserted them for Central Europe. The human inhabitants of these areas were faced with the challenge of desiccation.

Toynbee lists five different responses to this challenge. Some communities stayed where they were and tried to sit it out. But this was no ordinary drought and such communities suffered extinction. Others stayed where they were, but changed their way of life to suit the new conditions. These people became nomadic shepherds instead of hunters. The alternative to these responses was migration. Some communities migrated northwards, ultimately to be faced with the challenge of long cold winters. Others migrated southwards into the monsoon belt and 'came under the soporific influence emanating from the climatic monotony of the tropics'. The fifth response was the boldest of all and involved not only migration, but a complete change of life style as well. These were the people who set out to colonize the valleys of the Nile and the Tigris and Euphrates, at that time almost as impenetrable as the deserts they had left behind them were uninhabitable. These bold pioneers were the ultimate founders of the Egyptiac and Sumeric civilizations, and yet, at the time, they can have had little thought beyond the simple human urge for survival.

The fertile flood plain of the Nile occupies an area somewhat smaller than Britain. In the fourth millennium BC, both these areas were occupied by Neolithic communities which were, or had been, facing the challenge of new ground: clearing forests, draining marshes, or doing such other works as were necessary for the establishment of an agricultural economy. Towards the end of that millennium, Egypt emerged from prehistory into the first light of history. In this respect at least, the Egyptians were some three thousand years ahead of the British, the difference being due to the early development of writing in Egypt. Menes, King of Upper Egypt, conquered Lower Egypt in 3188 BC, and founded the first of a long line of dynasties of kings and pharaohs. Our knowledge of Egyptian civilization is based both on written records and archaeological remains. Comparison with Britain has to rely on the archaeological evidence alone.

The material equipment of the Neolithic communities in Egypt and Britain, though differing in detailed typology, was similar in its general character: polished stone and flint axes, flint arrowheads and sickles, stone saddle querns, simple pottery bowls. Perhaps the most significant difference between the Egyptian and British cultures of this early period is to be found in their burials. In Egypt, the dead were buried in simple grave pits dug in the sand. With them were buried personal ornaments, hunting implements, and pots of food and drink. In Britain, the disarticulated bones of the dead found their ultimate resting place in great communal chambered tombs, whose construction is far in advance of any contemporary structures preserved in Egypt. These chambered tombs served local communities for many hundreds of years. An interesting discussion of their place in Neolithic society has been presented by J.W. Hedges.[7]

The architectural development of tombs in Egypt began in the centuries following the establishment of the 1st Dynasty by King Menes. It coincided with the deposition of increasingly valuable grave goods and the consequent need for greater protection against tomb robbers. The early mastabas were constructed of mud brick in the general form of a house. They had a number of chambers besides the actual burial chamber and these held the equipment required for the afterlife. As time went on and the activities of the tomb robbers continued unabated, it became necessary to bury the grave goods in deeper chambers, often hewn out of the solid rock. Then, at the beginning of the 3rd Dynasty, King Zoser abandoned mud brick and was laid to rest in the first stone pyramid, the famous Step Pyramid.

The vast majority of Egyptian antiquities in the museums of the world have come from tombs. Of the houses of the people, the palaces of the kings, or even the great cities such as Memphis or Thebes, very little trace remains. The afterlife was going to last a great deal longer than the short earthly span, and the tombs had to be made to match. The tomb of a great man, often referred to as his castle of eternity, was designed to last for ever and was generally built of stone. It was also generously furnished with grave goods to meet all his material needs in the life beyond. His living quarters on earth had no need of such lasting qualities and were probably made of timber or mud bricks. Apart from the intrinsic quality of the artefacts themselves, this situation is almost perfectly mirrored in Britain in the early Bronze Age, for which most of the material in our museum collections comes from the excavation of burial mounds.

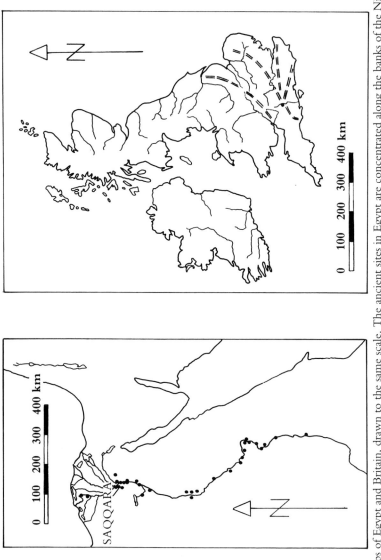

Maps of Egypt and Britain, drawn to the same scale. The ancient sites in Egypt are concentrated along the banks of the Nile, which provided a single arterial highway. In Britain, the net-work of communications (rivers and ridgeways) is much more complex. Stonehenge (S) occupies a relatively favourable position in the British communications network

During the fourth millennium BC, while the predecessors of King Menes were establishing their kingdoms in Upper and Lower Egypt, the Neolithic inhabitants of Britain seem to have lived in small local communities. In their communal chamber tombs, they all seem to have been equal in death and this is probably a fair indication of equality in life. Burial customs changed gradually during the third millennium, some of these changes being connected with the development of a class structure. The existence of kings and an associated aristocracy is most clearly indicated in the Wessex Culture burials, which are associated with the great period of Stonehenge III. By analogy with Egypt, albeit on a much smaller scale, we may perhaps surmise that, sometime towards the end of the third millennium BC, some unknown British equivalent of King Menes managed to establish his domination over neighbouring tribes and founded a dynasty, centred on Stonehenge, which lasted for several hundred years.

Salisbury Plain was probably not the most densely populated area in Britain at this time, but it combined a wide expanse of well-drained chalk with a central position in a radiating network of ridgeways and waterways. The Wiltshire Avon was the main route to the south coast and the west country. The Bristol Avon provided access to the Severn estuary and South Wales beyond. Further north, near Avebury, the river Kennett flows eastwards into the Thames at Reading, which can be followed upstream to the limestone ridge of the Cotswolds or downstream to the east. Apart from these waterways, the chalk of Salisbury Plain sends out ridges to the east and north-east, leading to the South Downs, the North Downs and the Chilterns.

In prehistoric terms, Salisbury Plain was a rich agricultural area. The chalk uplands were among the most popular environments for primary development. It was part of the relatively highly populated Lowland Zone but had, for many centuries, maintained close links with the Highland Zone. Cornwall was the main source of its stone axes and these were transported along the south coast to Christchurch Bay and then up the river Avon. The most remarkable record of contact with the Highland Zone of South Wales is the transport of the Stonehenge bluestones. How the first 'Stonehenge Kingdom' was established, we shall probably never know. Suffice it to say that overcoming the initial challenge of the environment and establishing a settled rural population had brought out characteristics of leadership, drive, ambition and courage. Men with these characteristics are always on the look-out for new challenges. Leaders endeavour to maintain their leadership, even when it is no longer a matter of life or death. Such were the men who had the bluestones brought from Mynydd Preselau to Stonehenge. Such a man was Ambrius, who ordered the building of Stonehenge III. Such were the 'Kings of Stonehenge'.

For all the similarities between the British early Bronze Age (particularly the Wessex Culture) and Egypt, however, the differences are vast. The Wessex Culture flourished for a mere five hundred years, and the architectural innovations at Stonehenge were never followed up. It is as if the seed of civilization was sown but failed to take root. In Egypt, on the other hand, it not only took root but lasted for three thousand years, far longer than any of the other civilizations discussed by Toynbee. King Zoser's Step Pyramid and its associated buildings were just the beginning of an architectural revolution. What was it that gave the Egyptian civilization its staying power and what prevented the development of a full scale civilization in Britain? Was the British civilization perhaps an arrested civilization, prevented by hostile environmental factors from achieving its full potential?

Once the initial challenge had been met and overcome, the fundamental geographical differences between the two countries took on a greater significance. The Egyptian civilization developed under the protection of a succession of ruling dynasties. King Menes established his rule over the two parts of Egypt by conquest. For the maintenance of such a kingdom, good communications are essential. In this respect, Egypt is served by a natural arterial waterway, the river Nile. Britain, on the other hand, is an area of the utmost geological and geographical complexity: highland areas, lowland areas, well drained limestone and chalk uplands interspersed with great expanses of intractable clay subsoils, sub-arctic conditions in the north, heavy rainfall in the west, and very indifferent communications except on a local scale. The obstacles against the establishment of an effective ruling dynasty, over even a small part of Britain, were enormous. Even the military might of the Roman Empire, served by its purpose-built network of roads, failed to bring the whole country under control.

CHAPTER 13

PREHISTORIC PILGRIMS AND THE TOURIST TRADE

The Neolithic ancestors of the builders of Stonehenge III had overcome the challenge of the environment in Britain. They had cleared forests, cultivated crops, bred livestock and established permanent settlements. Such activities were the very essence of Neolithic culture. So successful had they been that they were able to engage in such large scale non-productive projects as the building of chambered tombs and the construction of stone circles. They had also made considerable advances in several areas of applied and observational science. In mathematics, they had discovered how to construct circles, and also a variety of so-called 'flattened circles' and 'egg shapes', whose construction involved the use of right-angled (Pythagorean) triangles, such as the well known 3, 4, 5 triangle.[1] In geology, they had learned to recognize the type of stone best suited to a particular use, and had located and exploited, sometimes on a vast scale, the major sources of such raw materials.[2] This exploitation included the highly sophisticated mining of valuable seams of flint in the solid chalk rock – mining in every way analogous to the exploitation of particular coal seams in modern times. In engineering, they had mastered the use of ropes and levers for moving gigantic blocks of stone. In astronomy, they had discovered a good deal about the movements of the sun and moon and stars. And these are only the things that can be deduced directly from the material remains of their culture. How much more had they discovered that we shall probably never know?

The achievements of the Neolithic peoples of Britain were tremendous, but they were also universal. From the outer islands, beyond the shores of mainland Scotland, to the Scilly Isles and the white cliffs of Dover; from the Atlantic Ocean to the North Sea; the frontiers of knowledge were pushed forward in harmony, with such regional differences as we do discern being determined by geographical and geological factors, such as the distinction between the highland and lowland zones of Britain and the distribution of different rock formations. So what was

special about Wessex? Why did the Wessex Culture–Stonehenge III–
Hyperborean 'civilization' develop there and not anywhere else? In
answer to this question, Colin Burgess has pointed out that the Wessex
area had 'the biggest, best and most prestigious ritual and ceremonial
centres in the whole country'.[3] These included Silbury Hill, the largest
prehistoric mound in Europe; giant henges (banked enclosures), such as
Durrington Walls; the colossal stone circle complex at Avebury, with its
impressive stone avenues; the (uncompleted) double bluestone circle of
Stonehenge II; and the longest cursus (avenues flanked by banks and
external ditches) in the country, the Dorset cursus and the Stonehenge
cursus. These great monuments all pre-date the Wessex Culture and
therefore do provide a partial answer to the question. The Wessex
Culture developed because the Wessex area already had a long history of
doing things bigger and better than anywhere else. The question therefore remains the same but is moved further back in time. What was special about Wessex?

The social structure of Neolithic Britain seems to have been based on
small village communities; each self-sufficient, apart from some essential
raw materials which could only be obtained from a distance; each with
its communal burial mound (long barrow, chambered tomb), in which
there is no evidence of class distinction; each, with no problem of over-
population, at peace with the neighbouring communities. 'Decentral-
ization was total, with all decision-making taken right down at the
local commune level. . . . The neolithic was a period of minimal government.'[4] So what was it that set the people of Wessex on the road to
central administration, Stonehenge III, the Wessex Culture, and a
dynasty of kings with contacts as far away as Greece?

Geoffrey of Monmouth has only one answer to this question: military
success. King Arthur achieves his pre-eminence, first by subduing all the
other British kingdoms, and then by conquering the greater part of
Western Europe. Throughout Geoffrey's history, the bad times are due
to family feuds, civil war, foreign invasion and treachery, while the good
times follow the military successes of a strong king, who manages to
impose his rule over the whole country. Among the legendary early
kings of Britain, Ebraucus, the eponymous founder of York (Eburacum)
for example, invaded Gaul and came home victorious and laden with
gold and silver. He ruled for forty years and, having had no less than

twenty wives, died leaving twenty sons and thirty daughters. Not surprisingly, civil war broke out in the time of his grandson, Leif. Leif's son, Hudibras, restored order, and the peace lasted long enough for his son, Bladud, to indulge his taste for scientific experiment. Having founded the city of Bath and constructed the hot water baths there, he proceeded to make a pair of wings for himself, took to the air and crashed on the Temple of Apollo at Trinovantum, where he was smashed to pieces; thus ending a peaceful reign of twenty years and making way for his son Leir (Shakespeare's King Lear).[5]

The military conquest model fits the rise of Egyptian civilization perfectly. Menes, King of Upper Egypt, conquered Lower Egypt and, about 3200 BC, became the first ruler of the whole country. He heads Manetho's list of eight kings of the First Dynasty and, after a long and successful reign, 'was carried off by a hippopotamus'.[6]

There is, however, little archaeological evidence that military activity played any part in the development of the Wessex Culture. The equipment of the 'warriors' of this period, spears, daggers, bows and arrows, were just as likely to have been used in the chase (hunting red deer or wild boar) as in warfare. The introduction of rapiers and swords, during the period following the demise of the Wessex Culture, and the accompanying spread of hill-forts across the country indicate the onset of a period of tribal unrest. The 'Age of Hill-forts', which was to continue throughout the succeeding Iron Age, stands in stark contrast to the peaceful 'Age of Stonehenge'.[7] Furthermore, the rich Wessex graves are totally lacking in material which could be interpreted as loot from military campaigns against their neighbours. The gold objects are of highly characteristic local workmanship, and there is not a single example of the beautiful lunulae which are so widespread in Scotland and Ireland. The same applies to the amber spacer bead necklaces and the total lack of the equivalent jet necklaces of north-eastern England.[8]

Diodorus has nothing to say about the military prowess of the Hyperboreans, but a great deal about their temple and their religion; and, perhaps significantly, refers to their kings as 'the kings of this city',[9] rather than kings of a whole country. Could it be that the rise of the Wessex Culture resulted from a religious conquest, 'the biggest, best and most prestigious ritual and ceremonial centres',[10] rather than a military one? In this context, it is worth referring once more to Homer's 'Hymn

Oblique aerial view of Avebury from the north-west

to Delian Apollo' and recalling the words of Leto, Apollo's Hyperborean mother:

> If you (Delos) have the temple of far-shooting Apollo, all men will bring you hecatombs and gather here, and incessant savour of rich sacrifice will always arise, and you will feed those who dwell in you from the hand of strangers; for truly your own soil is not rich.[11]

This is saying, in effect, that building a great temple may be a thoroughly sound investment, immeasurably more valuable than good agricultural land. Again, in Homer's 'Hymn to Pythian Apollo', the Cretan sailors who have been waylaid by Apollo to serve as ministers in his new temple, wonder how they are going to survive in such a barren land. Apollo hastens to reassure them:

> Though each one of you with knife in hand should slaughter sheep continually, yet would you always have abundant store, even all that the glorious tribes of men bring here for me. But guard you my temple and receive the tribes of men that gather to this place, and especially show mortal men my will, and do you keep righteousness in your heart. But if any shall be disobedient and pay no heed to my warning, or if there shall be any idle word or deed and outrage as is common among mortal men, then other men shall be your masters and with a strong hand shall make you subject for ever. All has been told you: do you keep it in your heart.[12]

This is a further assurance that the investment in a temple to the god Apollo is sound, provided that it is well served by its priests. Profit from the investment depended on providing a good service to the people.

When the plans for Stonehenge III were being drawn up, Avebury stood in all its colossal magnificence no more than 27 km (17 miles) to the north; unspoilt by intrusive village houses; untouched by Christian stone breakers; still in almost mint condition after some five hundred years of use; an example which an ambitious young temple architect in Wessex, at the beginning of the second millennium BC, could hardly afford to ignore. And yet to anyone who has visited both sites, preferably one after the other, the contrast could hardly be more complete.

Quite clearly, Merlin did not try to build another Avebury. There would have been little point. Avebury had once and for all secured its place in the prehistoric equivalent of the Guinness Book of Records, with the greatest diameter, the heaviest stones, the largest number of stones, the longest stone-lined avenues, the most complicated arrangement of circles within circles. That had all been done. Avebury was without question the greatest monument of its kind. Stonehenge III is something totally different. It is not just another stone circle; it is a building; it is architecture. It is not smaller than Avebury because it was built on a tight budget. As we have seen, in an earlier chapter, nothing could be further from the truth. It cost a fortune. Stonehenge III was constructed with such wonderful precision that it is hard to believe it was not designed with equal care to meet clearly defined needs. In modern terminology, it must surely have been purpose built.

Stonehenge III should be viewed as the prehistoric answer to Avebury. For all its great size and awe-inspiring atmosphere, Avebury must have had its defects, and these will have been far more evident four thousand years ago than they are today. Where Stonehenge III differs from Avebury, we must therefore look for ways in which the Stonehenge version might be an improvement on Avebury. Apart from the architectural details, the most obvious difference between Avebury and Stonehenge is their relative sizes. The great outer stone circle at Avebury is large enough to contain a hundred circles the size of the Stonehenge sarsen circle! In what way was the small size of Stonehenge an improvement?

Avebury was a wonderful place for the people to gather. With its four great entrance causeways across the ditch, it was open to all. People converged on it from all directions and congregated in the huge enclosure. But what did they do when they got there? It is of course difficult to say. It was a long time ago. But then what do people do today when they get together? They meet old friends and relations, people they haven't seen since goodness knows when. They talk about their families and bring each other up to date on new babies, new wives or husbands, old parents who are not well enough to travel, older grandparents who may have died. And they talk about the weather. No British gathering would be complete without a full discussion of the weather and its consequences, the terrible winter, the floods, the failure of this crop or that, the leaking roof; or perhaps the wonderful summer and the promise of an early harvest. Or maybe they talk about hunting and fishing, and exchange tall stories about the ones that got away. And of course there is always sport. Yes, people talk. And then there is the pleasure of eating and drinking together. Some may go to the pub for a drink and emerge much later and much merrier. Others open their sandwiches and flasks of tea and have a picnic on the grass. Four thousand years ago the details would have been different, but the general effect was probably very much the same.

But, you may be thinking, Avebury was a great temple and the people gathered there for religious festivals. So they did. And this is where the priests come in. What did *they* do when all the people were assembled? What indeed? One might well ask 'What could they do?' And the answer might come back 'Very little.' The success of Avebury was its capacity to encourage and accommodate a vast throng of people. But this very success posed its own biggest problem: crowd control. It must have been enormously frustrating. At the great festivals, when crowds of people gathered from all the outlying districts, the priests were virtually powerless, quite unable to communicate with the masses. The people probably thoroughly enjoyed the festivals, but the priests may well have felt that they were no longer in control; and loss of control would have suited neither priests nor rulers.

Stonehenge III overcame these problems in one sweep of its masterly design. By a drastic reduction in the diameter of the circle and the spacing between adjacent stones, a clear division was established between the priestly area inside the circle and the popular area outside. The priests could perform their (secret) rites undisturbed by the crowds outside, even at festival times. The people could talk and picnic as much as they liked, outside the circle. Then, when it became necessary to communicate with the people, the chief priest or the king, or someone with the authority to represent them, could climb a ladder to the top of the great trilithon and stand high above the crowd, able to see and be seen by all, to be heard by all. Others in authority might also have stood on the other trilithons. Those in authority, whether material or spiritual, could stand high above the mass of the people and command attention. By a stroke of architectural genius, power had been restored and was to be retained in the hands of a ruling aristocracy for another five hundred years.

If Stonehenge III was not built as a local community temple, and all the evidence suggests that it was not, then it must have been intended as 'a place of pilgrimage', a temple to which people would travel from far and wide, perhaps for particular festivals, perhaps at less regular intervals, perhaps once in a lifetime. And the pilgrims are likely to have brought gifts with them (sheep or cattle or grain), possibly intended as sacrifices or gifts to the gods, but probably (judging by Homer's 'Hymns to Apollo', quoted above) serving for the upkeep and enrichment of the temple and its priests. The Stonehenge III–Wessex Culture–Hyperboreans had discovered the value of the 'tourist trade'. Over three thousand years later, their descendants in Glastonbury Abbey boosted their town tourist trade by the 'discovery' of the tomb of King Arthur in their very own graveyard, at a time when they were in desperate need of funds for rebuilding the Abbey, following a disastrous fire in 1184. This was described by Professor R.F. Treharne as 'a superb advertising stunt':

> In the golden age of forgery, here was the master-forgery of all! Perfectly timed and staged, on any grounds other than morality and religion it deserved to succeed, and succeed it did, and has gone on succeeding down to our own day.[13]

We know what drew the medieval pilgrims to their favourite shrines: tombs of the saints, holy relics, sites where the martyrs had suffered; and

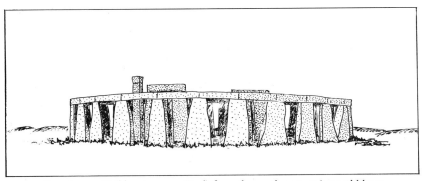

Stonehenge III (bluestones omitted) from the south-east, as it would have
appeared to a contemporary observer standing on the bank

if any of these had a reputation for miraculous healing, so much the better. With the murder of Archbishop Thomas à Becket in 1170, Canterbury Cathedral became the most important destination for pilgrims in Europe outside Rome itself; and, within a very short time of his death, there was abundant testimony of miraculous cures associated with him:

> For both in the places where he suffered and where he rested before the high altar when awaiting burial, as also in the place where he was buried, the paralysed are cured, the blind see, the deaf hear, the dumb speak, the lame walk, those sick of various diseases are healed. . . . I would not ever have presumed to write in this way, unless what I saw with my own eyes had not made me absolutely certain of what I say.[14]

St Thomas à Becket is still, nearly eight hundred years after his death, a major factor in Canterbury's tourist trade. Part of the secret of a successful tourist trade was, and is, the link between a place and some famous 'hero' of the past (religious or secular, historical or legendary): Shakespeare at Stratford, Sir Walter Scott at Abbotsford, Robert Bruce at Bannockburn, Lady Godiva at Coventry, Robin Hood in Sherwood Forest and Nottingham, and of course King Arthur at Glastonbury. The tourist trade may also be encouraged by special events, such as the Edinburgh Festival, the York Mystery Plays and the modern Glastonbury Pilgrimage; or even by a lone piper playing at the roadside, surrounded by the haunted grandeur of Glencoe. By visiting such places we strengthen our links with the past and reaffirm our national or cultural identity. What was it that drew our prehistoric ancestors to Stonehenge?

The men who were responsible for promoting Stonehenge III as a place of pilgrimage or a tourist attraction were in a unique position. What they were doing had never been done before. In a country which had, for well over a thousand years, been inhabited by people whose lives were centred on their own small agricultural communities, they were able to provide something larger: a sense of history, a sense of belonging, of national identity, of continuity with a past beyond the confines of their own 'parish'. The first pilgrims, marvelling as people have marvelled ever since, at their first sight of the great temple, would have been a captive audience for the orators towering above them on their lofty platforms. They would have heard how the young men of years gone by had journeyed across the sea to the sacred mountain, and returned with great stones which they set up in honour of their ancestors; how Merlin, with almost magical skill had built the temple as they saw it standing before them; and probably too how people had been cured of their ailments through the healing virtues of particular stones. The genealogy of the kings would have been recited, probably taking the ancestry of Ambrius back to an origin of irreproachable nobility among the gods. As time went on more names would have been added to the king list: perhaps Uther, who saw the great comet shaped like a dragon, after which he was named Utherpendragon; perhaps King Arthur himself; perhaps the now nameless occupant of the great Bush Barrow burial.

The pilgrims would have witnessed the public part of the temple ritual and, though we have no idea what this may have been, it is likely to have been larger, more colourful and more impressive in every way than anything they had ever seen in their local temple. They would have seen the sun rise, heard the priests singing, listened to the playing of the cithara, joined in the dancing round the circle of stones, made new friends and promised to see them again. Julius Caesar claimed that he came and saw and conquered. These early pilgrims came and saw and were conquered. They had become, in a very real sense, Stonehenge people. They went back to their homes irrevocably changed by the 'Stonehenge experience'. They told their friends what they had seen and heard, and each succeeding year the pilgrimages grew larger, drawing people from further and further afield, all bringing their gifts to the temple.

The kings, as Diodorus recorded, were kings of a city, apparently with no claim to be rulers of the whole or even a large part of Britain; but their influence spread far beyond the bounds of their own small kingdom, as far indeed as the fame of their great temple could carry it. They did not overcome their neighbours on the field of battle or subject them to their rule by force. They simply absorbed them into their own cultural heritage, and made sure that the hub of that culture was Stonehenge itself. And they grew rich on the proceeds.

CHAPTER 14

WHO WAS KING ARTHUR?

'Arthur of Britain', the longest chapter in Geoffrey of Monmouth's history, contains not a single mention of Stonehenge. The preceding chapter, 'The House of Constantine', ends with the burial of Utherpendragon, Arthur's father, at Stonehenge; and the next chapter, 'The Saxon Domination', starts with the reign of Constantine, Arthur's cousin and heir, and soon has him dead and buried at Stonehenge. Had Arthur not been mysteriously carried off to the Isle of Avalon to have his wounds healed, he too would surely have been buried alongside the other members of his dynasty.

In the early chapters of this book it was shown that Arthur's place in the history of British resistance to the Saxons is becoming increasingly difficult to maintain. In subsequent chapters, it has been suggested that some of the stories about Merlin, Ambrosius and Vortigern, all set by Geoffrey within a century-and-a-half of the departure of the Romans, find a more suitable place in the period of Stonehenge III and the Bronze Age Wessex Culture. Can the same be done for Arthur?

In order to answer this question, we have to treat Geoffrey's Arthur analytically, identifying the component parts of the story and gradually removing the later accretions to reveal what might remain of the original. Once it is accepted that the story is not, in its origin, a single continuous narrative about one man, it is not difficult to analyse it. The divisions listed below are intended as a basis for the discussion which follows.

1 Arthur and the Saxons
2 Arthur and the Picts and Scots
3 Twelve years of peace
4 Arthur in Gaul, Part I
5 Nine years of peace
6 Arthur in Gaul, Part II

7 Arthur and the plenary court

8 Arthur in Gaul, Part III

9 Arthur and the Giant of Mont Saint Michel

10 Arthur in Gaul, Part IV

11 Arthur and Mordred

'Arthur and the Saxons' is the Arthur of Nennius and the twelve battles. This is the Arthur who, in essence, has found his way into the history books of post-Roman Britain and has been the popular inspiration for much archaeological excavation at sites such as Cadbury Castle, sometimes hopefully referred to as Cadbury–Camelot.[1] This Arthur has been fully discussed in an earlier chapter and found to be somewhat lacking in historical substance.

The two periods of peace add up to a total of twenty-one years, a figure undoubtedly originating in the *Annales Cambriae*, where this is the number of years separating the battles of Badon and Camlann.

'Arthur in Gaul' is probably, as we have already seen, the result of attaching Arthur's name to the military exploits of Magnus Maximus in the late fourth century. There is no other period of British history in which this story makes any sense at all.

'Arthur and Mordred' has its source in the *Annales Cambriae*, where Arthur and Mordred are both recorded as having been killed in the battle of Camlann. Mordred's treachery at home provided Geoffrey with a very necessary device for removing Arthur from Europe, just in time for a return to something approaching the reality of the Dark Ages in his final chapter on the Saxon domination.

Geoffrey's problem with this collection of material relating to Arthur was how to arrange it chronologically so that it made the most sense. Given the basic assumptions that all the stories are historical and that they all relate to the same Arthur, Geoffrey's choice of the beginning and end of the sequence was more or less inevitable. Let us now see how he put the rest of the story together.

The fairly brief account of Arthur's campaign against the Picts and Scots might be accounted for in several ways. Geoffrey was well aware that the Saxons had been brought in to help the Britons ward off the persistent attacks from these 'traditional enemies'. It would have been clear to him, therefore, that the defeat of the Saxons could not have ensured the peace and prosperity of the kingdom unless the Picts and Scots had also been subdued. It would thus be possible to view this part of the story as a piece of historical fiction, invented by Geoffrey to make his narrative more convincing. It could on the other hand be derived from an otherwise unknown source, perhaps duplicating the battle in the Caledonian Wood, one of Arthur's twelve battles recorded in the histories of both Nennius and Geoffrey. On the other hand, it might belong with the campaigns of Magnus Maximus before his attack on Gaul.

Several things suggest that the campaign against the Picts and Scots was invented by Geoffrey. The first is that he not only defeated the Picts and Scots, but also conquered the whole of Ireland, as well as Iceland; feats which can have had not the slightest basis in the history of the fourth, fifth or sixth centuries. Secondly, the victories against the Irish, particularly, are somewhat stereotyped. When Gilmaurius, the King of Ireland, arrived with a fleet of ships and 'a huge horde of pagans' to assist the Picts and Scots, Arthur turned his army on them and 'cut them to pieces mercilessly and forced them to return home'.[2] The following summer, he invaded Ireland:

> The moment he landed, King Gilmaurius, about whom I have told you before, came to meet him with a numberless horde of his peoples ready to fight against him. However, when Arthur began the battle, Gilmaurius's army, which was naked and unarmed, was miserably cut to pieces where it stood, and ran away to any place where it could find refuge.[3]

These battles against the Irish are very reminiscent of Utherpendragon's expedition to Ireland (presumably also invented by Geoffrey) to collect the stones of the Giant's Ring from Mount Killaraus. In Uther's time, 'there reigned in Ireland a young man of remarkable valour called Gillomanius', who called his people to arms and assured them that 'as long as life remains in my body they shall not steal from us the minutest fragment of the Ring'.[4] These very soon proved to be empty words:

> When he saw that the Irish were spoiling for a fight, Uther hurriedly drew up his own line of battle and charged at them. The Britons were successful almost immediately. The Irish were either mangled or

killed outright, and Gillomanius forced to flee.

The third reason for supposing the campaign against the Picts and Scots to have been invented by Geoffrey is that he uses it as an opportunity to give an account of some of the 'wonders of Britain'. The Picts and Scots had hidden themselves on the islands of Loch Lomond, hoping that these would prove a safe refuge. At this point in the story, Geoffrey points out that 'this lake contains sixty islands and has sixty streams to feed it, yet only one of these streams flows down to the sea. On these islands one can make out sixty crags, which between them support exactly the same number of eagles' nests'.[5] This is the first among the 'Wonders of Britain' collected by Nennius,[6] though he refers these phenomena to Loch Leven rather than Loch Lomond. After this digression, Geoffrey returns to his story. Arthur assembled a fleet of boats and besieged the Picts and Scots for fifteen days, after which they were reduced 'to such a state of famine that they died in their thousands'. At this point the Irish arrived on the scene, as described above.

When the battle was over, Arthur found his cousin, King Hoel of Brittany, walking by the side of the loch counting the rocks and the eagles' nests. Seeing how interested he was in such matters, Arthur told him of an even more remarkable pool not far from where they were standing:

It was twenty feet wide and the same distance long, and its depth was just five feet. Whether it had been shaped into a square by the artistry of man, or by nature, it remained true that, while it produced four different kinds of fish in its four corners, the fish of any one corner were never found in any of the others.[7]

From this part of Geoffrey's history, wonders would seem to have been one of Arthur's favourite topics of conversation. Quite oblivious of the dead and dying all around them, he went on to tell Hoel about the Severn Bore and a remarkable pool called Lin Ligua, which swallows up the waters of the incoming tide and then, as the tide ebbs away, 'the pool belches forth the waters which it has swallowed, as high in the air as a mountain.' Like the wonder of the Loch and its islands and eagles' nests, this wonder is also described by Nennius, but the wonder of the square pool is peculiar to Geoffrey's history. Whatever their origin, these wonders hardly seem appropriate to a traditional battle story.

Once Ireland and Iceland had been conquered, Arthur 'established the whole of his kingdom in a state of lasting peace and then remained there for the next twelve years'.[8] During this prolonged period of peace, his court developed its well known glamour:

> He developed such a code of courtliness in his household that he inspired peoples far away to imitate him. The result was that even the man of noblest birth, once he was roused to rivalry, thought nothing at all of himself unless he wore his arms and dressed in the same way as Arthur's knights. At last the fame of Arthur's generosity and bravery spread to the very ends of the earth; and the kings of countries far across the sea trembled at the thought that they might be attacked and invaded by him, and so lose control of the lands under their dominion.

When Arthur heard that he was so universally dreaded, this 'encouraged him to conceive the idea of conquering the whole of Europe'. Such is the rather contrived continuity between the two major, but originally quite unrelated, components of Geoffrey's story of King Arthur. So Arthur sailed for Gaul, marched almost unopposed to Paris, defeated Frollo in single combat, and entered Paris. He then set about conquering the rest of Gaul:

> He divided his army into two and put one half under the command of Hoel, ordering him to attack Guitard, the leader of the Poitevins. With the other half Arthur busied himself in subduing the remaining provinces which were still hostile to him. Hoel soon reached Aquitania, seized the towns of that region, and, after harassing Guitard in a number of battles, forced him to surrender. He also ravaged Gascony with fire and sword, and forced its leaders to submit.

Nine years passed. Once Arthur had subjected all the regions of Gaul to his power, he returned once more to Paris and held a court there. He called an assembly of the clergy and the people, and settled the government of the realm peacefully and legally.

He then proceeded to arrange for the government of the conquered territories by placing his chief followers in positions of responsibility, making Bedevere, his Cup-bearer, Duke of Normandy, and Kay, his Seneschal, Duke of Anjou. The nine years do not belong to this story at all. If you remove those three words, 'nine years passed', and join the two paragraphs together, you have a perfectly reasonable account of the subjection of the Gauls. The nine years were interpolated by Geoffrey to fit his story to the chronology imposed by the *Annales Cambriae*.

The story of Arthur in Gaul is then interrupted once more to make room for the description of Arthur holding court at the City of the Legions. Kings, princes and nobles from all over Britain and the adjacent islands were there, and many from more distant lands:

Once they are listed, there remained no prince of any distinction this side of Spain who did not come when he received his invitation. There was nothing remarkable in this: for Arthur's generosity was known throughout the whole world and this made all men love him.[10]

After the celebrations were over, while Arthur was busy distributing bishoprics among his favourite clergy, twelve messengers arrived, bearing an irate letter from Lucius Hiberius, which began as follows:

Lucius, Procurator of the Republic, wishes that Arthur, King of Britain, may receive such treatment as he has deserved. I am amazed at the insolent way in which you continue your tyrannical behaviour. I am even more amazed at the damage which you have done to Rome. When I think about it, I am outraged that you should have so far forgotten yourself as not to realize this and not to appreciate immediately what it means that by your criminal behaviour you should have insulted the Senate, to which the entire world owes submission, as you very well know.[11]

You might be forgiven for thinking that such a letter could hardly have been intended for King Arthur, whose generosity was such that he was loved throughout the known world! On the other hand, a king who had just overrun the whole province of Gaul would have presented a serious threat to the stability of the Roman Empire. The account of Arthur's court at the City of the Legions is completely out of place here. It seems to be an independent piece of Arthurian tradition, collected by Geoffrey and inserted in this part of his narrative. If it is removed, the story of Arthur in Gaul regains its continuity.

The reaction to this letter was immediate and unanimous, and plans were quickly drawn up for an attack on Rome itself. A few months later, Arthur set sail from Southampton for Barfleur, about 15 km east of Cherbourg, where the whole army was due to rendezvous. Almost as soon as he landed, Arthur heard news of a monstrous giant who had come up from Spain, snatched Hoel's niece Helena, and carried her off to Mont Saint Michel, a rocky islet rising sheer out of the sea near the border between Normandy and Brittany.[12] In the middle of the night, Arthur roused his faithful companions, Bedevere and Kay, abandoned his army, and set off to slay the giant. They were too late to save Helena, but found the giant at the top of the crag, standing by his fire, his face 'smeared with the clotted blood of a number of pigs at which he had been gnawing'. In the ensuing fight, the giant wielded a huge club while Arthur fought with his sword. When Arthur had slain the giant, they cut off its head and carried it back to their camp. There are many such folk tales about giants carrying off maidens, hurling huge rocks at their attackers, fighting with enormous clubs, and finally being slain by human heroes. Geoffrey's reason for including this story is explained when Arthur sets off from his camp. 'Being a man of such outstanding courage, he had no need to lead a whole army against monsters of this sort. Not only was he himself strong enough to destroy them, but by doing so he wanted to inspire his men.' And inspire them he did. 'The three returned to their tents with the head, just as dawn was succeeding to night. All their men crowded round them to gape at it and praise the man who had freed the country from such a voracious monster.'

We are now in a position to search Geoffrey's account of King Arthur for possible prehistoric fragments. There seems to be no evidence that Arthur had any military reputation at all before his name became attached to the late fourth-century 'British' invasion of Europe under Magnus Maximus. After that, the temporary success of the British resistance against the Saxons in the sixth century was also attributed to him.

Then, with his reputation as a military leader well established, it was but a small step to the entirely fictional invasions of Ireland, Iceland and Norway introduced by Geoffrey. The twelve- and nine-year periods of peace, in so far as they are historical at all, relate to the sixth century, and the story of Arthur the giant-killer is a folk tale with no possible pretence to historicity. If all these are removed from Geoffrey's chapter on King Arthur, we are left with just one unit to consider, namely Arthur's plenary court at the City of the Legions; but before considering this in detail, it is worth taking a brief look at some stories about Arthur that Geoffrey did *not* include in his history.

Arthur appears in the lives of a number of early Welsh Saints.[13] In the *Life of St Cadoc*, he demands a herd of red and white cattle from Cadoc and his monks, who have been giving sanctuary to a man who killed three of Arthur's soldiers. The monks, with divine help, produce the cattle, but when Arthur's men take them they turn into bundles of fern. In the *Life of St Carannog*, Arthur steals a magic altar belonging to the saint and tries to use it as a table, but everything he places on it falls to the ground. In the *Life of St Padarn*, he bursts in on the saint and demands a tunic which the patriarch of Jerusalem had given him. Padarn refuses to hand it over and, when Arthur persists, the ground opens up and he falls in. As history, these 'lives' leave a lot to be desired, but as Geoffrey Ashe points out, taken together they do indicate that 'the Welsh monastic tradition would seem to have been unfriendly to Arthur'.[14] Arthur also appears in several of the Welsh 'triads'. In one of these he goes off, together with Kay (*Cai*) and Bedevere (*Bedwyr*), on an unsuccessful pig-stealing expedition!

Arthur the great hero, the glorious king, has stories told against him too. Is it simply that no man can become great without making enemies, or is there more to it than that? Geoffrey Ashe, discussing the problem in the context of Arthur as a sixth-century military leader, suggested 'that he requisitioned church property to maintain his troops',[15] and thus came to be portrayed as a plunderer in the lives of the saints. An equally plausible explanation is that Arthur was actually a prehistoric 'hero', intimately associated in folk memory with pagan traditions; traditions which the early church was doing its utmost to stamp out. On this interpretation, it has to be admitted that the attempts to blacken his name have failed. But the Arthur who has survived has been converted to Christianity and progressively updated through each succeeding age. Does any trace of his prehistoric past survive?

Returning now to Geoffrey's description of the City of the Legions, we read of its pleasant situation on the River Usk, of its material wealth, its royal palaces and the gold-painted gables of its roofs. The city was famous for its two churches, one of them 'graced by a choir of most lovely virgins' and the other 'served by a monastery of canons'.[16]

After describing the city, which was 'famous for such a wealth of pleasant things', Geoffrey gives an impressive list of the kings and nobles who came to the court. Some of them are familiar from earlier parts of the history: the kings of Albany (Scotland), Venedotia (Gwynedd, North Wales), Demetia (Dyfed, South Wales), Ireland, Iceland, Gotland, Norway and Denmark. Others are nobles of medieval type, such as the earls of Gloucester, Worcester, Salisbury and Warwick. There were also the great churchmen, the Archbishops of York and London. Those who came from Gaul include his own appointments, Bedevere, Duke of Normandy, and Kay, Duke of Anjou, as well as his lately defeated enemies, such as Guitard of Poitou. Then, 'in addition to these great leaders', Geoffrey names many 'other famous men of equal importance: Donaut map Papo, Cheneus map Coil, Peredur map Peridur, Grifud map Nogord, Regin map Claut, Eddelui map Oledauc, Kynar map Bangan . . .' The impression is successfully conveyed that a court of Arthur's was an occasion that no one would willingly miss. When all were assembled, the King was conducted with due ceremony 'to the church of the metropolitan see':

> On his right side and on his left there were two archbishops to support him. Four Kings, of Albany, Cornwall, Demetia and Venedotia, preceded him, as was their right, bearing before him four golden swords. A company of clerics of every rank advanced before him, chanting in exquisite harmony.[17]

Meanwhile, the Queen was conducted in similar style 'to the church of the dedicated virgins'. In both churches, the organists and the choirs thrilled the visitors with the beauty of their music, and finally high mass was celebrated. This was followed by a great feast, or rather two feasts, one for the men in the King's palace, and one for the married women in the Queen's palace. Then, 'invigorated by the food and drink which they had consumed, they went out into the meadows outside the city and split up into groups ready to play various games'. There was a tournament, and there were contests in archery, throwing the javelin, putting the weight, and even (presumably for those who had not been invigorated by the feast) playing dice.

However we interpret the details, it is quite clear that this was a glorious occasion and that people flocked to Arthur's court from far and wide. Whatever its ultimate origin, the description of the court and its ceremonial and feasting was updated to appeal to Geoffrey's twelfth-century readers.

There is no reason to associate the splendour of Arthur's court with the sixth century. Apart from its general unlikeliness in that period, it is not directly associated with any of the sixth-century components of the Arthur story. As far as the fourth-century story of Arthur (Magnus Maximus) in Gaul is concerned, there is no more reason to treat the plenary court as part of that tradition than to suppose that Arthur (Magnus) really left his army at Barfleur and set off in the middle of the night on a giant-killing expedition! This leaves us with the possibility that the tradition of King Arthur's magnificent court is indeed the most ancient part of the whole Arthurian legend, the closest to the 'real Arthur'. It could represent a distant memory of a great prehistoric Arthur, a pagan Arthur that the Celtic church strove in vain to suppress. If that were so, and if the same tradition (without the accretion of battles against the Saxons and Gauls) was also present in France, it would go a long way to explaining the sudden explosion of Arthurian romances (largely centred around the court rather than the battlefield) in the later twelfth and thirteenth centuries.

The weakness of this interpretation is that it presupposes a lost source for Geoffrey's account of King Arthur's court. Geoffrey's current reputation as a historian is such that many would rather believe he invented the whole thing for the further glorification of his great hero-king. It is a 'chicken and egg' problem. Was Arthur's name attached to the exploits of Magnus Maximus in Europe and to the early sixth-century British successes against the Saxons because it was already a household name, the name of a great king in a golden age of long ago? Or did Geoffrey invent the magnificent court of King Arthur because a king who was such a conquering hero ought to be graced with a court of medieval magnificence?

A lost source, by its very nature, is not available for examination, so let us consider the possibility that Geoffrey invented the splendour of Arthur's court. In the whole of Geoffrey's history, the pre-Roman brothers Brennius and Belinus must rank as the most successful military leaders.[18] After much civil strife, they joined forces and invaded Gaul. Within a year they had conquered the whole of Gaul and invaded Italy. The Italians submitted, handed over hostages, and agreed to pay an annual tribute. Then the brothers set off to invade Germany, but the Italians broke their treaty and marched to the assistance of the Germans. The brothers gave up their attempt on Germany and returned to inflict a crushing defeat on the Italians. 'Once he had won this victory, Brennius stayed on in Italy, where he treated the local people with unheard-of savagery.' 'Belinus for his part returned to Britain and for the remaining days of his life governed his homeland in peace.' He engaged in many good works: he founded a city on the River Usk, later to be known as the City of the Legions; in Trinovantum (Geoffrey's London) he built 'a gateway of extraordinary workmanship, which in his time the citizens called Billingsgate, from his own name'; he ratified his father's laws throughout the kingdom, 'taking pleasure in the proper administration of his own justice'. As a result of his good government, 'there became available to the populace such an abundance of wealth as no previous age had ever witnessed and no subsequent era was ever to acquire.' If ever a king deserved a magnificent court, that king was Belinus; but, in this respect, Geoffrey failed him completely.

Apart from Arthur, the only other king whose court is mentioned by Geoffrey is Utherpendragon. This court is brought in by Geoffrey to provide a setting for the King to fall in love with Ygerna, the wife of Gorlois, Duke of Cornwall: an affair which resulted in civil war and, later, in the birth of their son, King Arthur. The King summoned all his nobles to a court in London to celebrate Easter 'with proper ceremony':

> They all obeyed, travelling in from their various cities and assembling on the eve of the feast. The King was thus able to celebrate the feast as he had intended and to enjoy himself in the company of his leaders. They, too, were all happy, seeing that he had received them with such

affability. A great many nobles had gathered there, men worthy of taking part in such a gay festivity, together with their wives and daughters.[19]

That is all. The next paragraph is devoted entirely to the King's infatuation with Ygerna, her removal from the court by Gorlois, and the King's fury at losing her.

It is evident, from Geoffrey's summary account of the court of Utherpendragon and the total absence of any mention of a court for so great and good and wealthy a king as Belinus, that his treatment of King Arthur's court is quite exceptional. Not only that, but the brilliance of Arthur's court is described twice. There is the full account of the plenary court at the City of the Legions, discussed above, and then there is Geoffrey's rather curious use of the fame of Arthur's court as a cause of his invasion of Gaul. Initially the people of other countries tried to emulate the manners and customs of Arthur's court, but gradually their admiration turned to fear; and as they became more afraid, Arthur became more ambitious until, in the end, he determined to conquer the whole of Europe.

To return to the possibility of a lost source for the tradition of Arthur's court, there is just one passage in his description of the City of the Legions, immediately after the two churches, which seems out of place in a piece of early twelfth-century fiction:

> The city also contained a college of two hundred learned men, who were skilled in astronomy and the other arts, and who watched with great attention the courses of the stars and so by their careful computations prophesied for King Arthur any prodigies due at that time.[20]

Geoffrey of Monmouth lived and worked in Oxford, which was one of the foremost centres of learning in the whole country but, in the early twelfth century, the University existed in embryonic form only. There were, to be sure, masters and students in Oxford at this time, as there were in many other cities such as Exeter, Lincoln and Northampton, but they had not yet developed any formal organization; they could not, in any sense, be referred to as universities or colleges. Furthermore, though astronomy was certainly taught in the medieval schools, it was not given the pre-eminence implied in this description. This reads like a piece of genuine tradition, which has not been medievalized beyond recognition; a piece of tradition, therefore, which may provide a vital clue to the real Arthur.

Stonehenge, in one of its many guises, was medievalized as the Cloister of Ambrius, a monastery of 300 brethren. This is the only other instance in the whole of Geoffrey's history (apart from military units) of a numbered body of men. Peel off the medieval camouflage and you have a college of 300 priests serving a temple which was devoted to the gods of the sky: a spherical temple; a temple round which the god dances at the spring equinox, till the rising of the Pleiades; a temple of the Hyperboreans, whose god/constellation Abaris rushes round the world with his arrow. The college of 200 learned men, devoted to the study of astronomy, would be no strangers at the Cloister of Ambrius or Stonehenge III; they would be quite at home among the Hyperboreans, studying the features of the moon and drawing conclusions about its topography and its distance from the earth.

If the college of 200 learned men is traced back to Stonehenge III, King Arthur must be transported with them back to the Wessex Culture and the City of the Hyperboreans, where visitors from far-off Delos and Athens were given a royal welcome. And when those visitors went home, they took with them stories about the magnificence of the sacred precinct, the wonders of the spherical temple, the playing on the cithara and the singing. Geoffrey of Monmouth described the court of King Arthur from the point of view of 'the home team'. Diodorus, writing more than a thousand years earlier described essentially the same thing from the point of view of 'the visiting side'. If we allow for the 'updating factor', the agreement between the two accounts is quite remarkable. Geoffrey had no need to invent a court for King Arthur, to which kings and princes from conquered territories came to do him homage. There really was such a 'court' to which people came from as far away as Greece, for, as Diodorus says, the Hyperboreans 'are most friendly disposed towards the Greeks, and especially towards the Athenians and the Delians, who have inherited this goodwill from most ancient times'.[21] And, as Geoffrey tells us, 'there was nothing remarkable in this: for Arthur's generosity was known throughout the whole world and this made all men love him.'[22]

If this interpretation is anywhere near the truth, then Arthur was one of a long line of kings in the 'Stonehenge Dynasty', a member of the ruling family known to Diodorus as the Boreades. In early times, the genealogy of these kings would have been recited at regular intervals and their history kept alive in the oral tradition. By analogy with the Egyptian king lists preserved by Manetho, most of them would have been mere names, without recorded deeds, and these would soon be forgotten when the dynasty itself finally collapsed. Just a few were of more lasting quality: Ambrius, who started it all by building his great new temple at Stonehenge, and Arthur the Great, whose reign was remembered with nostalgia as a golden age, an age when men could travel to the ends of the Earth and be proud to be British! Arthur: Bronze Age king and immortal legend.

CHAPTER 15

VORTIGERN: TYRANT KING AND THE END OF STONEHENGE

Stonehenge is unique. This is at once one of the most obvious and one of the most significant facts about it. There are many stone circles in Britain, but only one Stonehenge. There are many pyramids in Egypt, many Egyptian temples, many Greek temples, many Mayan temples, many ancient Hindu temples, many medieval cathedrals, many medieval mosques; but only one Stonehenge. Its very uniqueness seems to be a feature of the Wessex–Stonehenge III–Hyperborean culture that distinguishes it from the main-line civilizations. Imhotep's great stone building complex at Saqqara marked the beginning of a long period in which Egypt produced some of the greatest architecture of the ancient world. Merlin's Stonehenge initiated no such period of architectural achievement. The Wessex Culture produced one great building and one alone, in spite of the fact that it lasted some five hundred years; roughly equivalent to the period between the Norman Conquest and the dissolution of the monasteries. It has already been noted that the Wessex Culture came to a rather sudden and unexplained end. It now appears that, after such a splendid start with the construction of Stonehenge III, it showed a peculiar lack of architectural drive. In view of what was achieved by the generation that built Stonehenge III, this can hardly be attributed to a lack of resources, either of manpower or of raw materials. We should therefore look for a political explanation for this anomaly.

Diodorus, in his account of the Hyperboreans and their spherical temple, gives a possible clue to the problem: 'And the kings of this city and the supervisors of the sacred precinct are called Boreades, since they are descendants of Boreas, and the succession to these positions is always kept in their family.'[1]

Here we have a dynasty of kings ruling, one might say, by divine right as descendants of Boreas; a dynasty determined to maintain its hold on all the positions of power. You might think that this sounds pretty much like any other dynasty, and you would be right. The significant point here is that, if our analysis is anywhere near the mark, the power of the dynasty was actually vested in Stonehenge itself. In this situation, building temples elsewhere would dissipate that power and reduce the flow of pilgrims (and wealth) to the centre of the royal authority. Quite the reverse would be the case in conquered territories, where temples might be built to encourage the dissemination of the dominant religion and culture among the subject peoples, thereby gradually rendering them compliant.

Sooner or later, such an exclusive power structure is almost certain to lead to trouble. Disputes may arise within the ruling family itself if any of their number feel cheated of their birthright. Jealousy is almost inevitable when able and ambitious young men find themselves excluded from office simply because they were born into the wrong family. Furthermore, wealth and status tend to foster a desire for greater wealth and greater status; and a dynasty which may have been fairly benign in its early years is liable to become more and more oppressive. The resultant civil discontent provides a ready source of manpower for any challenge to the monarchy, whatever its origin.

In Geoffrey of Monmouth's history, just such a challenge to the monarchy is presented by Vortigern. Nennius and Geoffrey both portray Vortigern as an evil man: ambitious, ruthless, scheming, treacherous and immoral. In Geoffrey's history, he is also directly involved in the darkest day in the long history of Stonehenge, the massacre at the Cloister of Ambrius. If Arthur is the greatest hero of these histories, Vortigern is surely the most dastardly villain. Geoffrey's story of how he usurped the crown gives a taste of what is to follow.[2] His opportunity came with the death of Constantine (grandfather of King Arthur), leaving three sons: Constans, who was a monk, and Aurelius Ambrosius and Uther-pendragon, who were both still 'in their cradles'.

Vortigern persuaded Constans to abandon his holy orders and take the crown. None of the bishops was prepared to anoint a monk as king, so Vortigern performed the coronation ceremony himself. With Constans installed as a puppet king, Vortigern assumed the reins of power; but this was only the first step towards his real ambition, which was the crown itself. He then brought some Pictish soldiers into the king's household, on the pretext that they would be able to provide useful information in the event of a Pictish attack. He treated them with such favour that they were soon persuaded that he should be king. From this it was but a small step to seeing the death of Constans as the only way to achieve this end. After a night of heavy drinking, the Picts rushed into the king's bedroom, killed him, and carried his head back to Vortigern. Far from rewarding them for their service, he feigned the greatest distress, had the Picts executed for their crime, and then took advantage of it by assuming the crown himself.

According to Nennius,[3] Vortigern was not only polygamous, but also seduced his own daughter and had a son by her, thus incurring the wrath of St Germanus. Some time after the arrival of his Saxon allies, Hengest and Horsa, he became very drunk at a banquet they had given in his honour, and developed an uncontrollable passion for Hengest's daughter. So besotted was he that he gave Hengest the whole county of Kent for her. In the end, according to one story, Vortigern died 'with all his wives', when his 'whole fortress was suddenly destroyed by fire sent from heaven'. According to another version, 'when he was hated for his sin by all men of his own nation, mighty and humble, slave and free, monk and layman, poor and great, he wandered from place to place until at last his heart broke and he died without honour.'

Vortigern's chief claim to the attention of historians is his policy of enlisting the aid of Saxon troops to defend the country against the inroads of the Picts and Scots. For this policy, which followed current practice in other parts of the Roman Empire, he was reviled by later British writers, who blamed him for the Saxon domination of much of southern Britain. He is thus generally accepted as a genuine and important figure in the immediately post-Roman history of Britain. His career, as recorded by Nennius and Geoffrey, however, does not all belong to this period of history. As Leslie Alcock expressed it, 'Vortigern was already the villain of a developed cycle of fabulous tales, in which Ambrosius also figured as the boy without a father who confuted Vortigern's magicians.'[5]

By the time Nennius was writing, several different stories about Vortigern were in circulation. The account of his dealings with the

Saxons was taken from the Kentish Chronicle (*in Cantia*); the stories of his family life and death were abstracted from the *Life of St Germanus* (*a Sancto Germano*); and the story of the fatherless boy and the magicians was an entirely separate unit, the *Tale of Emrys* (*de Ambrosio*). In an attempt to combine these different elements into an intelligible history, Nennius employed the technique known today as 'cut and paste' and, fortunately for us, preserved the identity of the pieces. Thus we have the following sequence: (i) *Kentish Chronicle*, Part 1; (ii) *Life of Saint Germanus*, Part 1; (iii) *Kentish Chronicle*, Part 2; (iv) *Life of Saint Germanus*, Part 2; (v) *Tale of Emrys*; (vi) *Kentish Chronicle*, Part 3; (vii) *Life of Saint Germanus*, Part 3.

How many Vortigerns were there and when did they live? Which were genuine historical characters and which fabulous? Nennius, writing more than four-and-a-half centuries after the arrival of the Saxons, worked on the assumption that there was only one Vortigern. Geoffrey of Monmouth, three centuries later again, saw no reason to disagree with him. Gildas, writing much nearer the time,[6] failed to mention Vortigern by name at all, just as he failed to mention Arthur. He did however refer to a 'proud tyrant' who, with his council, decided to invite the Saxons over to combat his enemies in the north. The identity of this proud tyrant with Vortigern has been almost universally accepted. In essence, he is telling the same story as the *Kentish Chronicle*, though with a frustrating lack of the names of people and places.

The identity of Vortigern presents us with two problems. Firstly, his name is not really a name at all but a title, meaning something like high chief. A twentieth-century example of such a title would be the German word *Führer*, simply meaning leader, which Hitler transformed into something so terrible that even Vortigern looks positively tame by comparison. Secondly, with the Vortigern who brought in the Saxons, we reach the limit of any sort of continuous history that can be based on British sources alone. Nennius complained that 'the scholars of the island of Britain had no skill, and set down no record in books',[7] and, apart from oral tradition, Gildas, writing about AD 540, is our earliest source.

How much history would we know if we had no books and had to rely entirely on what our parents and grandparents told us? We would know about the two World Wars and the British Empire and Queen

Victoria. We might have heard a story about Nelson putting a telescope to his blind eye, so that he could ignore a signalled order. We might have heard the bards reciting 'Not a drum was heard, not a funeral note, as his corse to the rampart we hurried.' But the Napoleonic wars, to which these fragments of oral tradition relate, would have no real place in our knowledge of history. Oral tradition is a living art form and only becomes relatively stable when it is eventually captured in written form. History, in any continuous form, would extend no more than a hundred years or so before our own time. Earlier traditions would have been progressively modified or lost. Returning to the time of Gildas, in the sixth century, real continuous history would have been restricted to the troubles of the post-Roman period. The Roman occupation of Britain would have been a distant and hazy memory, associated with the decaying remains of the cities and towns, and anything earlier would have consisted of no more than disconnected legends and songs.

Vortigern's chief claim to a place in the history of the Wessex–Stonehenge III–Hyperborean culture is the tradition, preserved by Geoffrey of Monmouth, of his involvement (on the losing side) in the disaster at the Cloister of Ambrius, which we have already considered in connection with the end of Stonehenge.

While accepting that the Wessex Culture and the great age of Stonehenge together do not amount to a full-scale civilization, it was none the less instructive to consider a civilization model for their development. The same method may now be used to interpret the end of the age. For a human death, the causes may be considered under three main headings: natural causes, murder, suicide. What we are discussing is the cause of death of a culture. Burgess considered murder by invasion and, finding no evidence for any invasion, decided to settle for death by natural causes. For some reason, the possibility of suicide was never mentioned, though Toynbee found evidence for this in the deaths of many civilizations.

Toynbee traced the demise of civilizations to 'times of troubles', which often preceded the ultimate end by many centuries. Thus his Hellenic civilization, which included the Roman Empire, had its time of troubles in the last four centuries BC, starting with the outbreak of the Peloponnesian War in 431 BC. The establishment of the Roman Empire arrested the decay of the Hellenic civilization for several centuries, but death was already inevitable long before the barbarian hordes swept in. In Egypt, the time of troubles began about 2400 BC, towards the end of the great Pyramid Age and about four hundred years after the reign of King Zoser. The authority of the central government broke down and Egypt suffered some four hundred years of civil war and anarchy. There seem to have been several causes for this time of troubles: (i) the drain on the economy due to the excessive expenditure of generations of kings on their pyramids and other funeral buildings; (ii) the rise in power of a new hereditary nobility; and (iii) the excessive power of the priesthood.

The Great Pyramids and the Giant Sphinx of Giza have stood for 4,500 years in silent witness to the achievement of Egyptian civilization. To us today, they are probably the greatest among the wonders of the ancient world. Cheops and his brother Chephren, the kings for whom they were built, are also, by association, thought of as great. But this may not be how they were remembered by the Egyptians. According to Herodotus, writing about a thousand years later, 'the Eygptians can hardly bring themselves to mention the names of Cheops and Chephren, so great is their hatred of them; they even call the pyramids after Philitis, a shepherd who at that time fed his flocks in the neighbourhood.'[8] They are said to have closed the temples, enslaved the people, forced them to quarry and haul great blocks of stone for the construction of the pyramids, and generally reduced the whole country to a state of abject misery. There were legends too, like the story of how Cheops, 'when short of money, sent his daughter to a bawdy house with instructions to charge a certain amount of money'. She did as she was told, but in addition, 'asked each of her customers to give her a block of stone, and of these stones was built the middle pyramid of the three which stand in front of the great pyramid'.

It may be that the Wessex Culture–Stonehenge III–Hyperborean culture succumbed to a time of troubles from which it was never able to recover. In the archaeological record, the age of Stonehenge, recently described by Burgess,[9] is followed, almost without a break, by the age of hill-forts. The development of hill-forts used to be considered a peculiarly Iron Age phenomenon, but recent investigations have pushed their origin well back into the Bronze Age. Unlike some archaeological remains, there is no doubt about the function of hill-forts. They are clearly defensive sites, and defensive works are only undertaken when there is fear of attack. The distribution of hill-forts gives no indication of concern with an external enemy. Probably the earliest examples of defences against an external enemy in Britain are the late Roman forts of the Saxon shore. The implication is quite clear. The Age of Stonehenge was followed by a long period of civil unrest, in which every tribe need-ed to erect defences against attacks by its neighbours.

A dramatic change in religion also took place at this time. The Y and Z Holes at Stonehenge provide a striking example of the sudden end of the old megalithic religion. The gods in the sky were replaced by new gods in the living waters of the earth. In the archaeological record, their importance is indicated by the abundant deposits of later Bronze Age metal-work in river gravels and bogs, in many parts of the country. In keeping with the political climate of the time, a high proportion of the objects so deposited were bronze weapons: swords, daggers and spears.

A possible interpretation of the rather sudden end of the Wessex Culture may be summarized as follows: (i) a 'time of troubles' of internal origin; (ii) the downfall (possibly violent) of the 'Stonehenge Dynasty'; (iii) the abandonment of the old religion with which that dynasty had been associated. Such an interpretation would be consistent both with the archaeological evidence and with the civilization model.

If the Egyptians could hardly bare to utter the names of Cheops and Chephren, the Britons may well have felt the same way about the last member of the Stonehenge Dynasty. They may have called him Vorti-gern rather than have to utter his real name, or this (or its ancient equivalent) might have been a title he chose for himself, just as Hitler chose to be known as *Der Führer*, at the same time banning the use of the word in any other context apart from compound nouns. Whatever it was that finally stretched the endurance of Vortigern's people beyond the limit, the end of his reign was sudden and the end of his dynasty final. He fled to the hills but, no longer able to wield his customary authority, he could not command the engineers and the labour force he needed to build his defences. In his extremity, neither magician nor prophet could provide any comfort. As Merlin said to him, in Geoffrey's account, 'two different ways of dying threaten you and it is not easy to see which of the two you will avoid.'[10]

The archaeological evidence seems quite clear that the end was sud-den and complete. Can Geoffrey of Monmouth's account of the massacre at the Cloister of Ambrius give us any clues as to what really happened? At this stage of the investigation, one can only say 'it is worth a try'.

In Geoffrey's story, there are several factions in existence at the time of the massacre: Vortigern, the usurper, always uncertain of his position without the backing of his Saxon allies; the brothers, Aurelius Ambrosius and Utherpendragon, out of the country but, with a legitimate claim to the throne, a potential threat to Vortigern; the British aristocracy, about 460 counts and earls present at the massacre, according to Geoffrey; Hengest and his Saxons, friends of Vortigern but enemies of the Britons.

In the prehistoric context, Geoffrey's Britons represent the old order of the Wessex Culture, and his Saxons the later Bronze Age culture, which followed the demise of the Wessex Culture. Trouble must have been brewing for some time, with the people becoming restless under the ever increasing burdens imposed on them by the kings and high priests and other members of the ruling family. Vortigern, ambitious and greedy for power and wealth, made use of this rumbling discontent in his own climb to power, but his rule proved even more oppressive than that of his predecessors. The people were divided. Some supported Vortigern because he was in power, and any authority was preferable to anarchy. Others supported the rightful heirs to the throne and plotted to overthrow Vortigern. And yet others saw their only hope in a full-scale revolution, ridding the country once and for all of the whole rotten system.

Revolution is seldom a bloodless affair. One has only to think of the French and Russian revolutions of modern times. As far back in history as the written word will take us, bloodless revolutions have been exceptional. Let us suppose then that we are planning a revolution to overthrow the Stonehenge Dynasty. How could we go about it? There can be little doubt that Stonehenge itself would be the ideal setting, and a religious festival an equally ideal opportunity. On such an occasion, there would be the maximum concentration of those in authority (lay and priestly, from the king downwards) inside the sarsen circle, and the maximum concentration of the ordinary people outside it. The plotters, with daggers hidden about their persons, could surround their intended victims without arousing the slightest suspicion. They would work their way into positions as close to the sarsen circle as possible and then, at a signal from their leader, they would draw their daggers and close on their victims. Escape would be impossible. There are only thirty openings in the circle and each would be barred by an armed man as the killers moved in to do their work. It would be bloody. It would be quick. It would be witnessed by many, but few would wish to challenge the authority of the bloodstained daggers of the assassins.

According to Geoffrey of Monmouth, the massacre took place on the first day of May, a detail he is so unlikely to have invented that it must surely belong to his source, particularly as there is no other such date in the whole of the history. May Day is a widely recognized spring festival day, whose origins go back to ancient times, though as a calendar date in its present form, it cannot have existed in prehistoric Britain. What this precise date implies is that, in the traditional story, the massacre took place at a great festival in the spring and, at some time before Geoffrey of Monmouth incorporated it in his history, that festival had become identified with the May Day festival. In its original form, the story might well have referred to the festival of the vernal equinox. There is no possible means of knowing.

Having planned this revolution to the best of our ability and considered all the circumstances which might affect its outcome, let us suppose that it actually happened that way. What would its effect have been?

On the innocent bystanders, all those people who had simply come for the festival, the effect would have been devastating. Stunned, sickened, revolted, frightened, soon only too well aware that it was not just a terrible dream; that moment when the great Temple of Ambrius was defiled, when the king and all his priests and leaders lay heaped on the bloody grass; that moment of horror would never leave them. A sharp order from the leader of the assassins would break through the tension in the air. The bodies must be removed from the temple at once and buried without delay. Hesitantly at first, the people would move to obey the orders of their new masters. There would be no raising of great burial mounds as befitted the ranks of the dead. Their hastily cremated remains would be dumped in simple pits in the ground or, at best, as secondary burials in earlier barrows. If any event was ever going to be imprinted on the national memory, this was it. The Temple of Ambrius from that day onwards would for ever be associated with this terrible massacre, and with the heart-rending and unceremonious disposal of the victims.

In the longer term, violence would breed more violence. The bloody revolution would not just signal the end of 'the old order', the end of the Stonehenge Dynasty, but the beginning of 'a new order'. There would be survivors of the Stonehenge Dynasty, who for some reason had not been present at the temple and had thus escaped the assassins' daggers. These would now have to fight for their rights. If they could gather enough support, they might be able to avenge the deaths of those who fell in the massacre. There would soon be disagreements among the rebel leaders of their descendants. At the massacre that we have visualized, political ends would be achieved by the use of weapons of war. This would become the pattern for the future and would lead to the development of improved weapons and the construction of defensive banks and ditches round the villages. The country would be in a state of intermittent civil war. Things would never be the same again.

That is what would happen if the revolution had been carried out in the manner we imagined.

But the story of that massacre *was* imprinted in the national memory; and perhaps more significantly, Geoffrey preserved the name Killaraus, which he located in Ireland, without realizing that *Cill-arach* means the burial place at the field of slaughter. It is as if he had preserved the story of the massacre twice, once knowingly and once quite unconsciously. And, in the longer term, the sudden demise of the Wessex Culture *was* followed by a period in which weapons of war became more prominent and more lethal, a period in which hill-forts were built, in short, a period of civil strife. The Great Age of Stonehenge, the Age of Arthur, had come to an end.

NOTES

Chapter One

1. Ashe, 1968; Alcock, 1971; Morris, 1973
2. Translated by Lewis Thorpe (1966). The quotations given below are from the 1988 impression, pp. 217, 222, 225, 255. Further references to this volume are given in the form 'Geoffrey, p. 255'.
3. Barber, 1986, p. 37.
4. *The Great Historical, Geographical and Poetical Dictionary* is described on its title page as being 'A Curious Miscellany of Sacred and Profane History, containing in short, the Lives and most Remarkable Actions of the Patriarchs, Judges, Kings of the Jews . . . . The Genealogy of several Illustrious Families in Europe, The Fabulous History of the Heathen Gods and Heroes, The Description of Empires, Kingdoms . . . . The Whole being full of Remarks and Curious Enquiries, for the Illustration of several Difficulties in Theology, History, Chronology and Geography.' It had been through six French editions, the last of which was 'Corrected and Enlarged by Monsieur Le Clerk', who is described in the Preface as 'a Famous French Protestant Divine'.
5. Collingwood and Myres, 1936, 2nd edn, 1949 reprint, p. 324.
6. Ashe, 1968, chronological chart following introduction.
7. Alcock, 1971, p. 88.
8. Morris, 1973, p. xiii.
9. Dumville, 1977, p. 187.
10. Salway, 1981, 1985 reprint, p. 485.

Chapter Two

1. Translated by M. Winterbottom (1978), p. 28. Further references to this translation are given in the form 'Gildas, p. 28'.

2. Frere, 1987, pp. 368-70. Fifth-century Mediterranean pottery, such as occurs at South Cadbury, Tintagel, Glastonbury Tor, etc. (Alcock, 1971), seems to be generally absent from towns, though it has been found at Dorchester.

3. Translated by John Morris (1980), p. 35. Further references to this translation are given in the form 'Nennius, p. 35'.

4. The Latin *in regione Linnuis* has often, though not universally, been translated as 'in the district of Lindsey', Lindsey being the northern part of Lincolnshire.

5. The Latin *humeros suos* means literally 'his shoulders' but, as Alcock (1971, pp. 57, 71) points out, the Welsh *scuid* for shoulder is very similar to *scuit* for shield, and an error may well have occurred during oral transmission or at the time of translation.

6. Dumville, 1977, p. 188.

7. Alcock, 1971, pp. 61-8.

8. Williams, 1969, p. 67.

9. Harrowven, 1977, 1980 reprint, p. 236.

10. Opie and Opie, 1959, pp. 98-9.

11. Geoffrey, p. 51.

12. Dumville, 1977, p. 181.

13. Salway, 1981, 1985 reprint, pp. 401-4.

14. Gildas, p. 21.

15. Geoffrey, p. 141.

16. Geoffrey, p. 223.

17. Alcock, 1971, pp. 123-9; Dumville, 1977, p. 181.

18. Nennius, p. 45.

19. See footnote 5.

20. Hughes, 1973, pp. 236-7.

21. In one of the later manuscripts, dates (AD) were used from 1097 onwards (Hughes, 1973, p. 243).

22. The Latin text actually reads '*ab incarnatione Domini nostri Jesu Christi*', but there must have been a mistake at some stage in the

copying of this passage, as the consulship of Felix and Taurus was in AD 428.

23. Nennius, p. 39
24. Nennius, pp. 45-7.
25. Alcock, 1971, p. 88.
26. Alcock, 1971, p. 73.
27. Alcock, 1971, pp. 61-8.

Chapter Three

1. Geoffrey p. 51.
2. See chapter 1, note 4.
3. Nicholas Tolstoy, *The Quest for Merlin, London*, 1985; R.J. Stewart, *The Mystic Life of Merlin*, Routledge and Kegan Paul, 1986.
4. Nennius, pp. 26, 29-9, 31-2. *The Kentish Chronicle* is divided into three parts, separated by two parts of the *Life of St Germanus* and the *Tale of Emrys*.
5. Nennius, p. 32.
6. Geoffrey, pp. 165, 195.
7. Geoffrey, pp. 164-5, 195-8.
8. Giraldus Cambrensis, *De instructione Principum*, written about 1214. The passage is quoted (in Latin) by Skene (1867, p. 165, see also pp. xx, liv). Other accounts of this massacre are also given by Skene (1867, pp. 202, 298, 334, 341).
9. Gildas, p. 27.
10. Geoffrey, p. 294; Tatlock, 1950, pp. 39-40.
11. Chambers Twentieth Century Dictionary. Edinburgh, W. and R. Chambers, 1972.
12. Chippindale, 1983, 1985 reprint, p. 20.
13. Geoffrey, p. 72.
14. Tatlock, 1950, p. 40.

Chapter Four

1.   Diodorus, with translation by C.H. Oldfather, Vol. III, pp. 151-9.

2.   Diodorus, with translation by C.H. Oldfather, Vol. II, pp. 37-41. Further references are given in the form 'Diodorus II, p. 37'.

3.   Herodotus, *The Histories*, translated by A. de Selincourt, pp. 281-2. Further references are given in the form 'Herodotus, p. 281'.

4.   *Hesiod, the Homeric Hymns and Homerica*, with translation by H.G. Evelyn White, p. 431. Further references to this volume are given in the form '*Hesiod* etc., p. 431'.

5.   *Hesiod* etc., pp. 325-37.

6.   Severin, 1987.

7.   The Metonic cycle, whereby the full moon occurs on the same calendar date every nineteen years, was discovered by the Greek astronomer Meton in the fifth century BC.

Chapter Five

1.   Chippindale, 1983.

2.   Atkinson, 1956.

3.   Richards, 1991.

4.   Radiocarbon dates in the text are given in round figures as approximate 'calendar' dates BC. The dates were actually determined in years 'bp' (before the present), which are easily converted to years 'bc'. The distinction between raw radiocarbon dates 'bc' and calibrated radiocarbon dates 'BC' is an important one. Tree ring dated wood samples, particularly from the long-lived bristle cone pine of California, give radiocarbon dates which agree well with the tree ring dates for the last 2,000 years, but then become progressively too young, until by 4000 BC, they are about eight hundred years short of the tree ring

dates. Using such data, it is possible to calibrate the radiocarbon dates to give 'calendar dates', though agreement on the best calibration system has not yet been reached. A good discussion, with calibration curves, is given by Renfrew (1974, pp 20-30). Radiocarbon dates are quoted with a standard deviation and a reference number, which enables them to be looked up in the journal *Radiocarbon*. The dates used in the text are given below in their uncalibrated form:

antler pick from ditch: 2180 +/- 105 bc (I-2328)
antler pick from ditch: 2460 +/- 60 bc (BM-1583)
antler pick from ditch: 2440 +/- 60 bc (BM-1617)
antler pick from unfinished R hole: 1620 +/- 110 bc (I-2384)
femur of skeleton in ditch: 1765 +/- 70 bc (BM-1582)
antler pick in fill of sarsen ramp: 1720 +/- 150 bc (BM-46)
antler pick from Y hole: 1240 +/-105 bc (I-2445)
antler pick from avenue extension: 1070 +/- 180 bc (BM-1079)
antler pick from avenue extension: 800 +/- 100 bc (I-3216).

5. Cunnington, 1924.
6. 'The Bronze Age', in Renfrew (ed.), 1974, p. 195.

Chapter Six

1. Geoffrey, p. 196.
2. Thomas, 1923.
3. Kellaway, 1971.
4. Gould, R.A., 1979 (the rabbit-eared bandicoot itself is a perfectly genuine marsupial of the genus *Thalacomys*).
5. Atkinson, 1956, pp. 174-5.
6. Geoffrey, p. 196.
7. Tatlock, 1950, pp. 81-2.

Chapter Seven

1.   Piggott, 1938; many of the objects also illustrated in colour in Clarke et al, 1985.
2.   Atkinson, 1956, p. 84.
3.   See chapter 5, note 4.
4.   Atkinson, 1956, p. 162.
5.   Thom, 1967.
6.   Hawkins, 1965.
7.   Renfrew, 1968, p. 283.
8.   Richards, 1991, plates 12, 13, facing p. 81.
9.   Clarke et al, 1985, pp. 121-2.
10.   Coles and Taylor, 1971; Clarke et al, 1985, p. 114.
11.   Burgess, 1980, p. 99.
12.   Homer, *The Iliad*, translated by E.V. Rieu, 1950, 1979 reprint, pp. 23, 24, 46, 168, 169.
13.   Herodotus, p. 281.
14.   Childe, 1929.
15.   Piggott, 1938.
16.   Atkinson, 1956, p. 162.
17.   Harding and Warren, 1973.

Chapter Eight

1.   Barry and Corley, 1968, 1977 reprint, p. 359.
2.   Glob, 1969.
3.   Godwin, 1981, chapter 12.
4.   Godwin, 1981, chapter 8 and figure 47, pp. 134-5.
5.   Godwin, 1981, chapter 8.
6.   Godwin, 1981, p. 135.
7.   Godwin, 1981, p. 15.
8.   David Willey, 1991, 'Diplomatic freeze over glacier man', *The Observer*, Sunday 29 September 1991, p. 24. Now known as

Similaun Man and dated to about 3300 BC ('John Musty's Science Diary' *Current Archaeology*, 1992, 128, p. 350).

9. B. Huntley and I.C. Prentice, 1988.
10. Barry and Chorley, 1968 (1977 reprint), figure 1.13, p. 47.
11 Huntley and Prentice, 1988, figure 1.

Chapter Nine

1. Edwards, 1947, chapter 2.
2. Manetho, with an English translation by W.G. Waddell, pp. 40-5. Manetho, an Egyptian priest of the third century BC, wrote a history of Egypt in Greek. His works have only survived as more or less fragmentary and inaccurate quotations, mainly in the writings of Josephus, Africanus and Eusebius. In the passage quoted (from Josephus), there is no significant difference between the three sources.
3. Geoffrey, p. 167.
4. Geoffrey, pp. 167-8.
5. Geoffrey, p. 171.
6. Nennius, p. 31.
7. Geoffrey, p. 196.
8. Nennius, p. 33
9. Luke 2, 42-52.
10. 1 Kings 16, 34.
11. Wheeler, 1943, pp. 38-9.

Chapter Ten

1. Gowland, 1902, p. 74, fig. 25 (copied from Memoir III of the Archaeological Survey of Egypt, El Bersheh, pt i, pl xv); Edwards (1947, p. 217) gives the weight as 60 tons, but this seems excessive. Round figure estimates of weight, given originally in tons (Atkinson, 1956, Heyerdahl, 1958) have been con-

verted into tonnes without altering the figures.   The tonne (metric ton or kilo) is equal to 0.984 tons, so there would be little point in changing an estimated 50 tons (the heaviest stone considered) to 49.2 tonnes.

2.   Atkinson, 1956, pp. 107-10.
3.   Joussaume, 1988, pp. 102-3.
4.   Heyerdahl, 1958, pp. 121-7.
5.   Heyerdahl, 1958, p. 149.
6.   Joussaume, 1988, pp. 249-50.
7.   Atkinson, 1956, p. 115.
8.   Joussaume, 1988, p. 250.
9.   Atkinson, 1956, pp. 119-123.
10.   Gowland, 1902, p. 79; Fenton, 1984, p. 223.
11.   Atkinson, 1956, p. 122.
12.   Fenton, 1984, p. 222.
13.   Heyerdahl, 1958, p. 136.
14.   Atkinson, 1956, pp. 125-9.
15.   Heyerdahl, 1958, pp. 144-8.
16.   Atkinson, 1956, pp. 129-35.
17.   Herodotus, p. 179.
18.   Heyerdahl, 1958, pp. 142-6.

Chapter Eleven

1.   1 Kings, 6 and 7.
2.   Geoffrey, 195.
3.   Ekwall, Eilert, *The Concise Oxford Dictionary of English Place-Names*, 3rd edition. Oxford University Press, 1947.
4.   Hawkins, 1963; 1964; 1965.
5.   Hawkins, 1964; 1965, p. 176.
6.   Heggie, 1981, pp. 195-202.
7.   Atkinson, 1956, p. 28.
8.   Diodorus II, p. 41.
9.   Hawkins, 1965, p. 128.
10.   Hawkins, 1964.

11. Heggie, 1981, pp. 100-4.
12. *Hesiod* etc., pp. 335-7.
13. Acts 2, 4-13.
14. 1 Corinthians 14, 1-6.
15. *Hesiod* etc., p. 345.
16. *Hesiod* etc., p. 363.
17. Geoffrey, p. 196.
18. Nennius, p. 31.
19. Geoffrey, p. 171.
20. Diodorus II, pp. 39-41.
21. Herodotus, p. 282.

Chapter Twelve

1. Diodorus II, p. 39.
2. Burl, 1987, p. 92.
3. Castleden, 1987, p. 60.
4. Burgess, 1980, p. 45.
5. Atkinson, 1956, p. 10.
6. Toynbee, 1946.
7. Hedges, 1984, pp. 99-126.

Chapter Thirteen

1. Heggie, 1981, chapter 4.
2. Cummins, 1979; Cummins, 1983, pp. 177-181, 196-8.
3. Burgess, 1980, p. 103.
4. Castleden, 1987, p. 213.
5. Geoffrey, p. 78-81.
6. Manetho, pp. 27-33.
7. Burgess, 1980, pp. 157-9, 353-4.
8. Clarke et al, 1985, pp. 107-128.
9. Diodorus II, p. 41.

10.   Burgess, 1980, p. 103.
11.   *Hesiod* etc, p. 329.
12.   *Hesiod* etc, p. 363.
13.   Treharne, 1967, 1969 reprint, p. 101.
14.   Knowles, 1970, p. 21.

Chapter Fourteen

1.   Alcock, 1971. The suggestion that Cadbury Castle is the site of Camelot of the Arthurian court goes back to John Leland in the sixteenth century (Alcock, 1972, chapter 1).
2.   Geoffrey, p. 219.
3.   Geoffrey, pp. 221-2.
4.   Geoffrey, p. 197.
5.   Geoffrey, p. 220.
6.   Nennius, p. 40.
7.   Geoffrey, p. 220.
8.   Geoffrey, p. 222.
9.   Geoffrey, p. 225.
10.   Geoffrey, p. 228.
11.   Geoffrey, pp. 230-1.
12.   Geoffrey, pp. 237-41.
13.   Ashe, 1968, pp. 62-4.
14.   Ashe, 1968, p. 61.
15.   Ashe, 1968, p. 63.
16.   Geoffrey, p. 226.
17.   Geoffrey, p. 228.
18.   Geoffrey, pp. 90-100.
19.   Geoffrey, pp. 204-5.
20.   Geoffrey, pp. 226-7.
21.   Diodorus II, p. 39.
22.   Geoffrey, p. 228.

Chapter Fifteen

1. Diodorus II, p. 41.
2. Geoffrey, pp. 151-5.
3. Nennius, p. 29.
4. Nennius, p. 33.
5. Alcock, 1971, p. 359.
6. Gildas, p. 28.
7. Nennius, p. 9.
8. Herodotus, pp. 179-80.
9. Burgess, 1980, pp. 157-9.
10. Geoffrey, p. 186.

BIBLIOGRAPHY

Alcock, Leslie, *Arthur's Britain: History and Archaeology AD 367-634*, London, Allen Lane, 1971.

Alcock, Leslie, '*By South Cadbury is that Camelot . . .': The excavation of Cadbury Castle, 1966–1970*, London, Thames and Hudson, 1972.

Ashe, Geoffrey (ed.), *The Quest for Arthur's Britain*, London, Pall Mall Press, 1968.

Atkinson, R.J.C., *Stonehenge*, London, Hamish Hamilton, 1956.

Barber, Richard, *King Arthur: Hero and Legend*, Woodbridge, Suffolk, Boydell Press, 1986.

Barry, R.G. and Corley, R.J., *Atmosphere, Weather and Climate*, 3rd edn, University Paperback, London, Methuen, 1968.

Burgess, Colin, *The Age of Stonehenge*, London, J.M. Dent, 1980.

Burl, Aubrey, *The Stonehenge People: Life and death at the world's greatest stone circle*, London, J.M. Dent, 1987.

Castleden, Rodney, *The Stonehenge People: An exploration of life in Neolithic Britain 4700–2000 BC*, London, Routledge and Kegan Paul,1987.

Childe, V.G., *The Danube in Prehistory,* Oxford University Press, 1929.

Chippindale, Christopher, *Stonehenge Complete*, London, Thames and Hudson, 1983.

Clarke, D.V., Cowie, T.G. and Foxon, Andrew (eds.), *Symbols of Power at the time of Stonehenge*, National Museum of Antiquities of Scotland, Edinburgh, HMSO, 1985.

Coles, J.M. and Taylor, 'The Wessex Culture: a minimal view', *Antiquity*, 45, pp. 6-14.

Collingwood, R.G., and Myres, J.N.L., 1937, *Roman Britain and the English Settlements*, 2nd edn, Oxford, Clarendon Press, 1949

Cummins, W.A., 'Neolithic stone axes: distribution and trade in

England and Wales', in Clough, T.H. McK. and Cummins, W.A. (eds.), *Stone axe studies*, pp. 5-12. CBA Research Report, No. 23, 1979.

Cummins, W.A., 1983, 'Petrology of stone axes and tools', in Kempe, D.R.C. and Harvey, A.P. (eds.), *The petrology of archaeological artefacts*, pp. 171-226, Oxford, Clarendon Press, 1983.

Cunnington, H.H., 'The blue stone from Boles Barrow', *Wiltshire Archaeological and Natural History Magazine*, 42 (1924), pp. 431-7.

Diodorus of Sicily, with an English translation by C.H. Oldfather, Loeb Classical Library, Volumes II and III. London, William Heinemann, and Cambridge, Mass., USA, Harvard University Press, 1935 and 1939.

Dumville, David N., 1977, 'Sub-Roman Britain: history and legend', *History*, 62 (1977), pp. 173-92.

Edwards, I.E.S., *The Pyramids of Egypt*, London, Penguin Books, 1947.

Fenton, M.B., 1984, 'The nature of the source and the manufacture of Scottish battle-axes and axe-hammers', *Proc. Prehist. Soc.*, 50 (1984), pp. 217-43.

Frere, Sheppard, *Britannia: A History of Roman Britain*, 3rd edition, London, Routledge and Kegan Paul, 1987.

Geoffrey of Monmouth, *The History of the Kings of Britain*, translated with an introduction by Lewis Thorpe, London, Penguin Books, 1966.

Gildas, *The Ruin of Britain and other works*, edited and translated by Michael Winterbottom, London and Chichester, Phillimore, 1978.

Glob, P.V., *The Bog People: Iron-Age Man Preserved*, translated from the Danish by Rupert Bruce-Mitford, London, Faber and Faber, 1969.

Godwin, Sir Harry, *The archives of the peat bogs*, Cambridge University Press, 1981.

Gould, R.A., 1979, 'Exotic stones and battered bones', *Archaeology*, 32 (1979), pp. 29-37.

Gowland, W., 'Recent excavations at Stonehenge', *Archaeologia*, 58 (1902), pp. 38-119.

Harding, A. and Warren, S.H., 'Early Bronze Age faience beads from Central Europe', *Antiquity*, 47 (1973), pp. 64-6.

Harrowven, Jean, *Origin of Rhymes, Songs and Sayings*, London, Kaye and Ward, 1977.

Hawkins, G.S., 1963, 'Stonehenge decoded', *Nature*, 200 (1963), pp. 306-8

Hawkins, G.S., 1964, 'Stonehenge: a Neolithic Computer', *Nature*, 202 (1964), pp. 1258-61

Hawkins, G.S., *Stonehenge decoded*, London, Souvenir Press, 1965.

Hedges, John W., *Tomb of the Eagles: a Window on Stone Age Tribal Britain*, London, John Murray, 1984.

Heggie, Douglas C., *Megalithic Science: ancient mathematics and astronomy in Northwest Europe*. London, Thames and Hudson, 1981.

Herodotus, *The Histories*, translated by A. de Selincourt. London, Penguin Books, 1954.

Hesiod, the Homeric Hymns and Homerica, with translation by H.G. Evelyn White and appendices, London and Harvard University Press, Cambridge, Mass., USA, Loeb, Classical Library, William Heinemann, 1935.

Heyerdahl, Thor, *Aku Aku: the secret of Easter Island*, English translation, London, George Allen and Unwin, 1958.

Homer, *The Iliad*, translated by E.V. Rieu, Penguin Books, 1950.

Hughes, Kathleen, 'The Welsh Latin Chronicles: *Annales Cambriae* and Related Texts', Sir John Rhys Memorial Lecture, *Proc. Brit. Acad.*, 59 (1973), pp. 233-58.

Huntley, B. and Prentice, I.C., July temperatures in Europe from pollen data, 6000 BP', *Science*, 241 (1988), pp. 687-90.

Joussaume, R., *Dolmens for the dead: megalith building throughout the world*, English translation, London, B.T. Batsford, 1988.

Kellaway, G.A., 1971, 'Glaciation and the stones of Stonehenge', *Nature*, 233 (1971), pp. 30-35.

Knowles, David, 'Archbishop Thomas Becket: the Saint', *Canterbury Cathedral Chronicle*, 65 (1970), pp. 5-21.

Manetho, English translation by W.G. Waddell, London and Harvard University Press, Cambridge, Mass., USA, Loeb Classical Library, William Heinemann, 1940.

Morris, John, *The Age of Arthur: a History of the British Isles from 350 to 650*, London, Weidenfeld and Nicolson, 1973.

Nennius, *British History and the Welsh Annals*, edited and translated by John Morris, London and Chichester, Phillimore, 1980.

Opie, Iona and Peter, *The Lore and Language of Schoolchildren*, Oxford University Press, 1959.

Piggott, Stuart, 'The Early Bronze Age in Wessex, *Proc. Prehist. Soc.*, 4 (1988), pp. 52-106.

Renfrew, Colin, 1968, 'Wessex without Mycenae', *Annual of the British School at Athens*, 63 (1968), 277-85.

Renfrew, Colin (ed.), *British Prehistory: a new outline*, London, Gerald Duckworth and Co., 1974.

Richards, Julian, *Stonehenge*, London, B.T. Batsford/English Heritage, 1991.

Salway, Peter, *Roman Britain*, Oxford, Clarendon Press, 1981.

Severin, Tim, *The Ulysses Voyage: Sea search for the Odyssey*, London, Century Hutchinson, 1987.

Skene, William F. (ed.), *Chronicles of the Picts, Chronicles of the Scots, and other early memorials of Scottish History*, Edinburgh, HM General Register House, 1867.

Stone, E.H., 'The method of erecting the stones of Stonehenge', *Wiltshire Archaeological and Natural History Magazine*, 42 (1924), pp. 446-56.

Tatlock, J.S.P., *The Legendary History of Britain*, Berkeley and Los Angeles, University of California Press, 1950.

Thom, A., *Megalithic sites in Britain*, Oxford University Press, 1967.

Thomas, H.H., 'The source of the stones of Stonehenge', *Antiquaries Journal*, 3 (1923), pp. 239-260.

Toynbee, Arnold J., *A Study of History*, Abridgement of Volumes I-VI by D.C. Somervell and Geoffrey Cumberlege, London, Oxford University Press, 1946.

Treharne, R.F., *The Glastonbury Legends: Joseph of Arimathea, The Holy Grail and King Arthur*, London, The Cresset Press, 1967.

Wheeler, R.E.M., 1943, 'Maiden Castle, Dorset', *Report of the Research Committee of the Society of Antiquaries of London*, XII, 1943.

Williams, A.H., *An introduction to the History of Wales*, Vol. II; The Middle Ages, Part I, 1063-1284. Cardiff, University of Wales Press, 1969.

INDEX

Italicized figures refer to illustrations.

Abaris, 35, 129, 161
Abbotsford, 147
Abiram, 98
Achaean, *see* Greek
Achilles, 74, 76
Adriatic, 36, 78
Aegean, 34, *37*
Aegina, *37*, 38
Aeneas, 32
Africa, 51, 79
Africa, North, 134
Agamemnon, 74, 76–7
Agricola, 92
Albany (Scotland), King of, 157
Alcock, Professor Leslie, 8, 21, 165
Aldroenus, King of the Armorican Britons, 81
Alfred the Great, 8
Alps, 15, 85
Ambrius, 27, 117–18, 129, 138, 162
Ambrius, Cloister (Temple) of, 27, 29–33, 41,
    54–5, 57, 68, 89–90, 95, 98, 100, 117–18,
    161, 164, 167, 170–1
Ambrosius, 9–12, 17–18, 24, 25, 27, *28*, 58,
    89–90, 95–98, 117–18, 126–7, 129, 149,
    164, 171
Amesbury, 27, 31, 57, 62, 118
Andean civilization, 133
Andros, 36, *37*, 78
Annales Cambriae, 1–18, *19*, 20–1, 25, 150,
    154
Apollo, 36, 38, 39, 40, 77, 122, 125–6, 129,
    130, 143, 146
Apollo, Temple of, 77, 141
Aquilea, 16
Aquitania, 153
Arabia, 133
Ararat, Mount, 66
Arfderydd, battle, 20
Arge, 36
Argos, 77
Aries, 41

Artemis, 36, 125
Arthur, King,
— Age of, 3, 115, 117
— battles, 4–7, 10–13, 17–18, 20–2, 150–2
— 'Bronze Age king', 148, 161–2
— court, 3, 153, 157–61
— historicity, 3, 8
— invasion of Gaul, 10, 14–16, 153–5
— last of the Romans, 10
— legend, 22–3, 24–5, 33, 39, 41, 89–90,
    140, 147, 149, 156, 162, 164
— mobile cavalry commander, 7
— not mentioned by Gildas, 9, 166
— not mentioned by Diodorus, 129
— tomb, 8, 146
Arthur son of Petr, 22
Artuir son of Aidan, 22
Ashe, Geoffrey, 8, 156
Asclepios, 93, 122
Athenians, 35, 72, 74, 161
Athens, 36, *37*
Athos, 36, *37*
Atkinson, Professor R.J.C., 45, 47, 55, 57, 60,
    65, 101, 104, 105, 113, 121, 132
Atreus, 74
Aubrey Holes, *see* Stonehenge
Aubrey, John, 45
Aulus Plautius, 92
Aunjetitz, *see* Unetice
Aurelius, *see* Ambrosius
Australia, 65
Austria, 79
Autun, 4, 6
Avalon, Isle of, 149
Avebury, 107, 114, 137, 140, 144–5
Avon, River, 31, 62, 101, 134

Bacon, Francis, 91
Badon, battle, 7, 9–14, 17–18, *19*, 21, 22, 150
Baltic, 79
Bannockburn, 147

Barfleur, 155, 158
barrows, round, *54*, 65–6
barrows, long, 65–6
Bath, 141
Bath, battle, 3, 5, 12
Beaker people, 65
Becket, Thomas, Archbishop of Canterbury, 147
Bede, 14, 24
Bedevere, 154–7
Belinus, 159
Billingsgate, 159
Black Sea, 79
Bladud, 141
bluestones, glacial transport, 61–2, 64, 66
bluestones, *see* Stonehenge
bog people, 83
Bohemia, 79
Boles Barrow, 48, 65–6
Boreades, 40, 162, 163
Boreas, 35, 40, 163
Boudicca, 92
Bougon, 101
Brassas, River, battle, 10, 13
Brennius, 159
Brigantes, 92
Bristol, 134
Bristol Channel, 60, 62
British Empire, 166
Brittany, 57, 70, 79, 81, 155
Brogar, Ring of, 107
Bronze Age, 78–9, 82–6, 115, 135, 138, 149, 168, 170
Bruce, Robert, King of Scotland, 147
Brutus, 32, 67
Buckingham Palace, 121
Burgess, Colin, 57, 140, 167, 168
Bush Barrow, 69–71, 73, 148

Cadbury, *see* South Cadbury Castle
Cadwallon, 20
Caen stone, 58
Caer Legion, *see* Legion, City of
Caesar, Julius, 92, 148
Caledonian Forest, battle, 10, 12–13, 151
Caliburn, 4, 5
Callet, R.P., 102
Camelot, 7, 150
Camlann, battle, 5–6, 9, 17, 19, 21–2, 150
canoe, dug-out, 84
Canterbury, 147
Canterbury Cathedral, 58, 147

Cantscaul, battle, 20
Caratacus, 92
Carboniferous, 62
Cardiff, 62
Carn Alw, 60
Carn Meini, 60, 66
Carno, Mount, battle, 20
Carpathos, *37*, 38
Carystians, 36, 78
Carystus, 36, *37*, 78
Cassiopeia, 41, 129
Cassivelaunus, 92
Cat Coit Celidon, *see* Caledonian Forest
Cateyrn son of Vortigern, 26
Celts, 34
Cepheus, 129
Cheops, 168, 169
Chephren, 168, 169
Cherbourg, 155
Chilterns, 137
Chios, *37*, 38
Chippindale, Christopher, 45
Chretien de Troyes, 6
Christmas, 124
Chryses, 77
cithara, Hyperborean players, 39, 122, 123, 130
civilizations, 133–4
Claudius, 92
Clevedon, 62, *63*
climate, 82–6
Climatic Optimum, 75–6
Collingwood, R.G., 7, 10
Constans, uncle of King Arthur, 164–5
Constantine, grandfather of King Arthur, 165
Constantine, cousin and heir of King Arthur, 25, 149
Corineus, 32
Cornish, battle among, 20
Cornwall, 32, 34, 137
Cornwall, King of, 157
Cos, *37*, 38
Cosheston Group, 60, 66
Cotswolds, 137
Coventry, 147
Cretaceous, 62
Crete, *37*, 38, 65, 69
crop marks, 131
Cross of Jesus Christ, on Arthur's shield, 21
Cunnington, William, 48, 62, 65
cursus, 140
Cygnus, *128*, 129

Cynthus, Mount, 38
Czechoslovakia, 79

Dalriada, 22
Danube, River, 79
Decius, consul, 18
'Delian Apollo', Hymn, 38, 125, 143
Delians, 35, 72, 74, 78, 125, 129, 130, 161
Delos, 35–6, *37*, 51, 77–80, 125, 143
Demetia, King of, 95, 99, 157
Delphi, 125
Denmark, 6
Devon, 62
Devonian, 62
Diodorus Siculus, 34–6, 39–40, 51, 54, 55, 69,
    82, 84, 85, 86, 89, 118, 122–4, 129, 141,
    148, 162, 163
Dionysus, 38
Dodona, *37*
Dodonaeans, 36, 78
dolerite, spotted, 59–60, 60, *63*, 64–5
dolerite, 'unspotted', 60, 62, *63*, 64–5
Douglas, River, battle, 10, 12–13
dragons, red and white, 127
Dumville, D.N., 8
Durrington Walls, 132, 140
Dyfed, 59

East Anglia, 84
Easter, 124
Easter Island, 100, 101–2, *103*, 108–9, 110–11,
    112, *113*
Ebraucus, 140
eclipse prediction, 123
Edinburgh Festival, 147
Edwin, 20
Egypt, 70, 74, 93, 108, 112, 130, 134–7, *136*,
    138, 141, 168
Egyptiac civilization, 133, 134, 138
Egyptians, 93–5, 99, 100, 103–4, 105, 112,
    134–5, 162, 168
Elbe, River, 79, *80*
Eldol, Count of Gloucester, 27
Elfoddw (Elvudog), Bishop of Bangor, 10
Eliffer, 20
equinox, vernal, 40–1, 123–4
equinoxes, precession, 41
Eskimo (arrested) civilization, 133
Essex, 27
Euboea, 36, *37*, 78
Euphrates, River, 134
Europe, Central, 134

Exeter, 160

Felix, consul, 18
fens, 84
First World War, 166
Flat Holme, 62, *63*
France, King, *see* Henry IV
Freezland, 7
Frollo, 4, 16, 153

Galahad, 6
Garth Maelog, battle, 20
Gascony, 153
Gaul, 4, 6, 10, 15–16, 34, 140, 149–51, 153–5,
    157–60
Geoffrey of Monmouth, 3, 5–8, 12–17, 21–3,
    24–7, 29–33, 39, 40, 48, 54–5, 57, 58–9, 60,
    64, 67–8, 81, 89–90, 91, 93, 95–7, 98–9,
    117–18, 126–7, 140, 149–61, 164–7,
    169–72
Geological Survey, 59, 60, 61
George III, 13
Germany, 79
giants, 32, 58, 150, 155
Giant's Castle, Causeway, Cave, Grave, House,
    Quoit, 32
Giant's Ring, 27, 29, 32, 58, 67–8, 99, 151
Gildas, 8–12, 16–18, 22–4, 31, 89–90, 117,
    166, 167
Gillomanius, King of Ireland, 29, 151
Gillmaurius, King of Ireland, 151
Giraldus Cambrensis, 30
Giza, 168
glacial erratics, 61–2, 64
glacier man, 85, 179
Glamorganshire, 60
Glastonbury, 8, 83, 84
Glastonbury Abbey, 146
Glastonbury Pilgrimage, 147
Glein, River, battle, 10, 13
Glencoe, 147
Gloucester, Bishop of, 27
Godiva, Lady, 147
gold, Wessex, 69–70, 73–5, 141
gold, Mycenaean, 74, 76
Gorlois, Duke of Cornwall, 159–60
Gotland, 5
Gowland, Professor William, 107
Gratian, Western Roman Emperor, 15, 16
Greece, *37*, 38, 69–70, 76, 78–9, 85–6, 89,
    140
Greeks, 35–6, 39–41, 51, 69–70, 78, 83, 86,

122–3, 130, 132, 161
Greenland, 82
Guinevere, 5
Guinnion Fort, battle, 10
Guitard, leader of the Poitevins, 153
Gwenddolau, son of Ceidio, 20
Gwrangon, King of Kent, 26

Hamlet, 91
Hawkins, Professor G.S., 118, 123
healing stones, 58–9
Hecateus, 34, 122
Hedges, J.W., 135
Hehil, 20
Helena, niece of Hoel, 155
Hellenic civilization, 133, 167
henges, 140
Hengest, 24–7, 165, 170
Henry IV, King of France, 14
Herodotus, 35–6, 38, 39, 78, 104, 113, 125,
    129, 168
Hesiod, 38
Heyerdahl, Thor, 100–2, 104, 108, 110
Hiel the Bethelite, 98
Highland Zone, 66, 137
hillforts, 141, 168
Hillforts, Age of, 141, 168
Hitler, Adolf, 166, 169
Hoel, King of Brittany, 81, 152, 153, 155
Holwell, 61
Homer, 23, 38, 39, 74, 91, 125–6, 141, 143,
    146
Horsa, 24, 26, 165
Hudibras, 141
Huntingdon, Henry of, 45, 115
Hyde Park, 121
Hyperboreans, 34–6, 38, 39–41, 69, 71, 72, 74,
    76, 78, 79, 89, 122–5, 129, 130–1, 132, 140,
    141, 143, 146, 161, 163, 167, 168
Hyperoche, 36

Ice Age, 133–4
Ice Age, Little, 82
Iceland, 5, 153, 157
Iceni, 92
Ictis, 34
Ida, Mount, 65
Iliad, 38, 74, 76–7, 91
Imbros, 37, 38
Imhotep, 93–5, 98, 99, 122, 163
Indus civilization, 130, 131
Insall, Squadron Leader, G.S.M., 131

Ionians, 125
Ireland, 5, 29, 33, 57, 58, 67–8, 73, 99, 141,
    151, 153, 157, 172
Irish, 151–2
Iron Age, 141, 168
Italians, 159
Italy, 15

Jehutihetep, 100
Jericho, 98
Jerusalem, 98, 117
Jesus, 98, 124
John, King, 12
Jurassic, 62

Kaercaradduc, 27
Kaerliudcoit, battle, 12
Kaiser, the, 14
Kakovatos, 70
Kay, 154, 156, 157
Kellaway, G.A., 61–2
Kenn, 62
Kenneth MacAlpin, 30
Kennett, River, 137
Kent, 26–7, 165
Kentish Chronicle, 26, 31, 98, 166
Kildare, Killala, Killare, 67
Killaraus, Mount, 58, 67–8, 99, 151, 172
Knossos, 37, 69–70, 126

Lake, 62
Lake District, 62
lake villages, 84
Lancelot, 6
Laodice, 36
Lapland, 7
Layamon, 6
Legion, City of, 154–7, 159–60
Legion, City of, battle, 20
Leif, 141
Leir (King Lear), 141
Lemnos, 37, 38
Lesbos, 37, 38
Leto, 38, 77, 125, 143
Lincoln, 160
Lincoln, battle, 12
Lindow man, 83
Lindsey, battle, 10, 12
Lin Ligua, 152
Liverpool, Roman Catholic Cathedral, 119
Llewellyn the Great, 12
Loch Leven, 152

Lock Lomond, 152
Lowland Zone, 137
Lucius Hiberius, 154
Lycea, 35

Madagascar, 100, 102, 104, 115
Maelgwn, 18, 20
Magnus Maximus, 15–17, 90, 150, 151, 155, 158
Maiden Castle, 98
Malian Gulf, 36, *37*, 78
Malory, Sir Thomas, 22
Manetho, 93–4, 141, 162
Marlborough Downs, 105
massacre at Stonehenge (prehistoric), 170–2
massacre of Britons by Saxons, 26–31, 33, 164
massacre of Picts by Scots, 29–30
Mayan civilization, 133
May Day, 171
Meare, 84
Mediterranean civilization, 34, 72, 130, 131
Medraut, *see* Mordred
Meigen, battle, 20
Memphis, 93, 135
Mendips, 62
Menes, King of Egypt, 134, 135, 137, 138, 141
Merlin,
— and the Giant's Ring, 29, 58, 64, 67, 95
— and the King's magicians, 95–7
— architect of Stonehenge, 89–2, 94, 144, 148, 163
— legend, 24–6, 33, 41, 95, 148
— mediumship, 97, 126–7
— oracle, 126–7
— prophet, 95–9, 126–7, 169
— virgin birth, 95–6, 97, 98, 99, 126
Meton, 40, 123–4
Miathi, 22
Middle East, civilizations, 130, 131
Middlesex, 27
Miletus, *37*, 38
Milford Haven, 61, *63*
Minoan civilization, 133
Mocetauc, battle, 20
Mohen, J-P., 101, 105, 112
moon, 39, 122–3
Moravia, 79
Mordred, 5, 21, 150
Morris, J., 8
Mycale, *37*, 38
Mycenae, *37*, 69–74, 76–9, 90

Napoleon, 14
Napoleonic Wars, 167
Naxos, *37*, 38
Necherophes, King of Egypt, 93
Nelson, 167
Nennius, 7, 10–15, 24, 30, 89–90, 91, 96–8, 99, 126, 150, 151, 152–3, 164, 165–6
Neolithic, 46, 65, 83, 108, 131, 135, 137, 139–40
Netherlands, 13
Newall, R.S., 123
Nile, River, 134, *137*, 138
Nomad (arrested) civilization, 133
North Downs, 137
North Sea, 79
Normandy, 155
Northampton, 160
Norway, 6, 156
Nottingham, 147
Nunney, 61, *63*

oceanic islands, 133
Oder, River, 79
Odysseus, 24, 39, 74, 76
Odyssey, 38, 91
Old Red Sandstone, 60–1
Olen of Lycea, 36
Opis, 36
Ordovician, 60
Orkney, 5, 107, 131
Ororoina, 101–2
Oxford University, 160

Pannonia, 15
Paris, 4, 153
Parnassus, Mount, *37*, 125
Paros, *37*, 38
Passover, 124
peat bogs, 83–4
Pedro Atan, Mayor of Easter Island, 101–2, 108–9, 110–11, 112
Pegasus, 129
Peloponnesian War, 167
Pembrokeshire, 59–61, *63*, 65
Pencon, battle, 20
Perseus, 41
Percival, 6
Philitis, 169
Phoebus, 38
Picts, 15, 20, 26, 29–30, 149, 150–2
Piggott, Professor S., 71–2
pine, bristle cone, 71–2

Pisces, 41
plague, 20
Pleiades, 40–1, 51, 123, 161
Poland, 79
Politetes, King of Bithynia, 5
pollen analysis, 83–6
Polynesian (arrested) civilization, 133
Pope, the, 121
Preselau (Prescelly, Preseli), Mynydd, 59–61, 64–7, 120, 138
preselite, 60
Priam, 76
Ptah, 93, 95, 98
Pyramid, Great, 104, 113–14, 168
Pyramid, Step, 92–3, 135, 138
Pythean Apollo, Hymn, 125–6, 143
Pytheas, 34, 39

Quantock Hills, 62

radiocarbon dating (*see also* Stonehenge), 71, 72, 83, 84, 85, 102, 132, 176–7
Rameses II, 93
Rano Raraku, 102
Reading, 137
Redhorn Hill, 106, *106*
Renfrew, Professor Colin, 72
Rhone, mouth of, 34
rhyolite, 60
Richards, Julian, 45
Rillaton, 70
Robin Hood, 147
Rochester Cathedral, 58
Rochford, 69
Roman Empire, 135, 155, 165, 167
Roman period, 83
Romans, 4, 6, 89, 92, 149, 167
Rome, 4, 154
Russia, 7

sacred sites, 65–7
Sahara, 133
St Albans Cathedral, 58
St Cadoc, 156
St Carannog, 156
St Davids, 17, 22
St Germanus, 98, 166
St Michael's Mount, Cornwall, 34
St Michel, Mont, Brittany, 150, 155
St Padarn, 156
St Paul, 91, 125
Salisbury, 27, 101

Salisbury Plain, 59, 61–2, 67, *106*, 131–2, 137
Salway, P., 8
Samos, *37*, 38
sandstone, micaceous, 60, 61–2, 67, 120
Saqqara, 92–4, 99
Saracens, 7
sarsen stones (*see also* Stonehenge), 48
Saxons, 3, 5, 7, 9, 21, 24, 25, 26, 29–30, 32, 68, 97, 118, 149–51, 156, 158, 165–6, 170
Saxony, 79
Scandinavia, 84
Schliemann, Heinrich, 38
Scone, 30
Scotland, 29, 73, 141
Scots, 15, 26, 29–30, 149–52, 165
Scott, Sir Walter, 147
Scyros, *37*, 38
Scythia, 35, 78
Second World War, 166
Selyf son of Cynan, 20
Senni Beds, 60, 66
Sertorius, King of Libya, 5
Severin, Tim, 38
Severn Estuary, 137
Severn bore, 152
Shakespeare, William, 91, 141, 147
Shapwick, 84
Sherwood Forest, 147
Silbury Hill, 140
Silesia, 79
Similaun glacier, 85, 179
Sinic civilization, 133
Solomon, Temple of, 117
Somerset, 62
Somerset levels, 83
South Cadbury Castle, 7, 150
South Downs, 137
Southampton, 155
Spain, 15, 142–3
Speakers' Corner, 109
Sphinx, 157
Stone, E.H., 96–9
Stonehenge,
— Altar Stone, *56*, 59, 60–1, 64, 67, 119–20
— architecture, 49, *50*, 51, *52*, 53, 71, 90–4, 132
— astronomy, 118–20, 122–4
— Aubrey Holes, 45, *46*, 54, 123
— avenue, 51, 57
— bank, *46*, 54, 132
— bluestones, 46–9, 55, 59–67, 138
— building costs, 100, 113–15

— cremation cemetery, 45, *46*, 54
— ditch, *46*, 48–9
— ditch burial, 48
— erecting stones, 110–11
— Great Age, 89, 137, 167, 172
— Heel Stone, 55, *56*
— purpose, 117–29
— Q, R Holes, 47, 49
— radiocarbon dates, 46, 47, 49, 51, 57, 71
— raising lintel stones, 111–13
— sarsen stones, 49–51, 59, 107–8
— shaping of stones, 107–9
—Slaughter Stone, 55, *56*
—Station Stones, 55, *56, 123*
— Stonehenge I, 45, *46*, 83
— Stonehenge II, 46–7, 49, 66, 140
— Stonehenge III, 49–53, 69, 72, 90–1, 110, 113–15, 119, 121, 132, 137–40, 143–6, 149, 161, 163, 167–8
— Stonehenge Dynasty, 169–70, 172
— transport of stones, 100–7, 114
— Y, Z Holes, 55, *56*, 57, 169
Stratford-on-Avon, 147
Stukeley, William, 48
Sumeric civilization, 133, 134
sun, 40
sunrise, midsummer, 67, 119–20
sunset, midwinter, 67, 120
Sussex, 27

Talorgan, 20
Tatlock, J.S.P., 31
Taurus, 41
Taurus, consul, 18
temple, spherical, 39–40, 51, 69, 89, 122, 163
Tenians, 36, 78
Tenos, 36, *37*, 78
Thames, River, 137
Thanet, 26
Thebes, 135
Theodosius, consul, 18
Thersites, 76
Thomas, H.H., 59–62
Tigris, River, 134
tin, Cornish, 34
Tintagel, 7
Totnes, 32
Toynbee, Professor Arnold, 133–4, 167
trackways, timber, 83–4
Treharne, Professor R.F., 146
Treves, *see* Trier

Triassic, 62
Trier, 16
Trinovantum (London), 141, 159
Trojan War, 39
Troy, 38–9, 74, 76, 132

Ulysses, 39
Unetice Culture, 79, *80*
Usk, River, 157, 159
Utherpendragon, 25, 95, 99, 148, 149, 151, 159–60, 164, 170

Valentinian, Emperor, 16
Valentinian, consul, 18
Valerian, consul, 18
Vendotia, King of, 157
Vespasian, 92
Victoria, Queen, 166–7
Vienna, 79
Vikings, 82
Virgin Mary, image on Arthur's shield, 10, 13, 21
Vitalinus, 18
Vortigern, 18, 24, 26–7, 89, 95–6, 149, 164–7, 169–70
Vortimer, son of Vortigern, 26

Wace, 6
Wales, North, 62, 73
Wales, South, 60, 62, *63*, 66, 137
Wallop, battle, 18
Wessex Culture, 57, 69–75, 77, 79, 86, 132–3, 137, 138, 140, 141, 146, 149, 161, 163, 167, 168–70
Western civilization, 133
Weston-Super-Mare, 62
Westonzoyland, 62, *63*
Wheeler, Sir Mortimer, 98
William the Conqueror, 8
Williams, Professor A., 12
Wiltshire, 69–70
Winchester Cathedral, 58
Woodhenge, 91, 131

Ygerna, mother of King Arthur, 159–60
York, 140
York, battle, 12
York, Grand old Duke, 13–14, 31
York Mystery Plays, 147

Zeus, 77
Zoser, King of Egypt, 92–3, 135, 138, 168